The BHS
Training Man
■ FOR THE ■
PTT
Incorporating the
UKCC Level 2

The BHS
Training Manual
FOR THE
PTT
Incorporating the
UKCC Level 2

The British Horse Society
Registered Charity No. 210504

Islay Auty FBHS

Updated and expanded by

MARGARET LININGTON-PAYNE, MA(ED),BHSI

KENILWORTH PRESS

Copyright © 2009 British Horse Society

First published in the UK in 2005
by Kenilworth Press, an imprint of Quiller Publishing Ltd

This edition published 2009

British Library Cataloguing-in-Publication Data
A catalogue record for this book
is available from the British Library

ISBN 978 1 905693 26 9

The information in this book is true and complete to the best of our knowledge. All recommendations are made without any guarantee on the part of the Publisher, who also disclaims any liability incurred in connection with the use of this data or specific details.

Drawings by Dianne Breeze
Layout by Sharyn Troughton
Printed in Great Britain by Bell & Bain Ltd., Glasgow.

Kenilworth Press
An imprint of Quiller Publishing Ltd
Wykey House, Wykey, Shrewsbury, SY4 1JA
Tel: 01939 261616 Fax: 01939 261606
E-mail: info@quillerbooks.com
Website: www.kenilworthpress.co.uk

Contents

Picture Acknowledgements

All line drawings are by **Dianne Breeze**.

Picture sources
The author and publishers wish to acknowledge the following books as sources for the illustrations:

- **The BHS Manual of Equitation**, Consultant Editor Islay Auty FBHS, published by Kenilworth Press

- **Learn to Ride with the BHS**, by Islay Auty FBHS, published by Kenilworth Press

- **The BHS Instructors' Manual for Teaching Riding**, by Islay Auty FBHS, published by Kenilworth Press

How to Use this Book

The aim of this book is to provide students working towards the Preliminary Teaching Test with detailed guidance on how to prepare thoroughly for the examination and how to achieve UKCC Level 2 should they wish to do so.

You will find that the book echoes the structure of the syllabus and follows a clear pattern. The syllabus itself is divided into **elements** under specific headings (e.g. class lesson on the flat, written paper, etc.). For each element you will find information on '**What the assessor is looking for**', followed by advice on '**How to become competent**'.

The syllabus elements marked **C** (compulsory) cover work which will almost certainly be assessed or covered in some aspect in the exam. Those marked **S** (supporting) include work which may be assessed during the exam and which is considered as supplementary, enhancing the basic standard of knowledge required from you.

It is important to realise that you can never achieve competence purely by reading a book, or indeed any number of books. Books can enhance and assist you in your study, but teaching riding is a very practical subject. It is up to you to ensure that your competence develops from practical experience, through observing lessons given by well-qualified or experienced teachers, and by developing your own practical teaching skills in as many controlled supervised situations as you can.

Understanding the PTT Exam

You will by now have had some experience of taking exams yourself, either through Pony Club tests, in taking your BHS Stage 1 and 2, or NVQ assessment and verification, but the PTT is likely to be the first time that you are assessed as a teacher.

It is therefore helpful during your training if you have had some genuine experience of riders who are novices or even complete beginners. You can gain this experience in the following ways:

- By observation in a commercial riding school of weekly riders of different ages and abilities.

- By leading novice children or adults in lessons under the supervision of a qualified instructor. This could be done in association with a commercial riding school.

- By helping novice or beginner riders to lead their horses to the school, adjusting stirrups and girths and helping them again at the end of a lesson.

- By watching as many lessons as you can, given by more experienced instructors.

- By taking your generic BHS UKCC Level 1 endorsed qualification.

These opportunities allow you to appreciate just how limited the complete beginner's experience might be. It should help you to remember never to assume that a rider knows something already and to ensure that you teach every aspect of a lesson.

Study the syllabus carefully and discuss with your trainer where your weak areas might be, as well as your strengths. Make a plan for developing confidence and competence in the areas where you feel less secure. For example, if you feel nervous standing up and giving a short presentation, make sure that you take every opportunity to practise this by talking to groups of friends, family or informal gatherings so that you develop confidence. Confidence comes with practice and learning to teach takes time and practice.

You must feel confident about:

■ Projecting your own voice from the start of the lesson.

■ Teach according to what is happening in front of you, not to a stereotyped plan which may not apply to the pupils you have.

■ Adhering to clear basic principles such as good basic position, application of the aids and control and understanding of the horse.

■ Progressing the lesson in the way you believe is in the best interests of the class or individual, not because you think the assessors want to see you do something particular.

Your own presentation is important because it will give you an air of authority and image, which is important for an instructor/coach.

■ Make sure that you have a hat, whip and gloves close by so that in extreme cases you could ride a pupil's horse that was behaving badly. If you teach in your hat the chin strap may be undone so that you can speak easily. It is not necessary to carry a stick while teaching.

■ Dress as for previous exams (beige or fawn breeches, boots, shirt and tie and hacking jacket, have top coat or waterproof in case it is either cold or wet).

■ Your image should be neat, tidy and professional.

Typical exam turnout – neat, tidy and professional.

The assessor will be looking for competence in teaching correct basic principles. You must be able to:

■ Demonstrate self-confidence.

■ Show an ability to project your voice both indoors and outside, and maintain an audible voice throughout.

British Horse Society
Preliminary Teaching Test

PROGRAMME

8.15		Candidates assemble
		Please have your membership card ready in order that the assessor's can check your identity
8.30		Candidates briefing
9.00	1 - 2	Class lesson

After a maximum of 10 minutes assessment, discuss with the assessor the relevance of their pre-prepared lesson plan for 2/3 minutes

9.33		Finish lesson

Assessor invites feedback & reflection from candidate for approx 5 minutes. Feed back from riders 2/3 minutes.

9.00	7 -10	Classroom lesson (Lecture)
9.40	3 - 4	Class lesson (as above)
10.00	7 -10	Break
10.10	7 -10	Business knowledge questions
10.20	5 - 6	Class lesson (as above)
11.00	7 - 8	Class lesson (as above)
	1 - 6	Classroom lesson (Lecture)
11.40	9 -10	Class lesson (as above)
12.00	1 - 6	Break
12.10	1 - 6	Business knowledge questions
12.20		Teaching assessors bring all paperwork up to date
1.00		**LUNCH**
1.45	1 – 6	Lunge novice adult OR lead rein lesson for a beginner

(Note to Assessors and Centre:- 3 horses and riders for lunging. 3 horses and riders for lead-rein. Each assessor to do one candidate at a time)
After a maximum of 5 minutes assessment discuss with the Assessor the relevance of their pre-prepared lesson plan for 2/3 minutes After 20 minutes finish lesson Assessor invites feedback & reflection from candidate for approx 3 minutes Feed back from rider. 2 minutes Each candidate to have 25 minutes in total.

1.45	7 – 10	Teaching theory inc. accident procedure, sports psychology & child protection (60minutes)
3.00	7 – 10	Lunge novice adult 2 riders OR lead rein lesson for a beginner 2 candidates (as above)
3.00	1 – 6	Teaching theory inc. accident procedure, sports psychology & child protection (60 minutes)
4.00	7 – 10	Review with teaching assessors.
4.15	1 – 6	Review with teaching assessors.
	7 – 10	EXAM ENDS - results sent by post
4.35	1 – 6	EXAM ENDS - results sent by post
		Assessors complete paper work.

- Control your riders.

- Develop a rapport with your riders and encourage them to think for themselves and give you feedback.

- Progress your pupils to some benefit and improvement.

- Deal with simple situations as they arise (e.g. if a horse is apparently lame, you must comment on it; if a rider appears worried, you must attempt to address the problem).

- You must demonstrate a competence to discuss basic lesson plans for a variety of teaching situations.

If at any stage the assessor feels that you are drifting away from developing your lesson satisfactorily, then he or she may suggest that you take a certain path (e.g. introduce jumping position if you are giving a jump lesson and have spent rather too long on the flat). Always regard this as a help, not an interference – the assessor is aiming to help you to show your best and is usually more aware of the time limitations of the exam than you are.

On arrival at the exam centre for your Preliminary Teaching Test, you will be briefed by the chief assessor, who will introduce the team of assessors for the day. The day's events will be explained to you and there will be a programme clearly listed for your benefit. The chief assessor will give each candidate a piece of paper on which there will be:

- A number.

- A subject for your class lesson (which will either be a lesson on the flat or one involving poles or jumps).

- A subject for your presentation.

- Whether you are required to give a lead-rein or a lunge lesson.

You need to be aware that an overall 'pass' is dependent on achieving success in a minimum number of Compulsory and Supporting elements – see the specimen results on page 12. An 'x' in a box adjacent to an element means that you have been unsuccessful in that element.

PRELIMINARY TEACHING TEST

Result Sheet

The British Horse Society
Registered Charity No. 210504

Equestrian
Qualifications GB
Limited

Examination Centre: _____ Date: _____

Chief Assessor: _____

_____
Candidates Name and Number

PASSED / FAILED

* NB – A total of 8 crosses or more throughout whole of the PTT constitutes a fail

To be read in conjunction with the assessment criteria detailed in the PTT syllabus

Preliminary Teaching Test					Unit code number S3PTTE				
Topic	C = Compulsory element S = Supporting element X adjacent to an element number indicates an unattained element								X - adjacent to the minimum required shows an unattained topic
	Element	Element	Element	Element	Element	Element	Element	Element	Min. Required
Class lesson on the flat Or Class lesson using ground poles or jumps	1.1.1 C	1.1.2 C	1.2.1 S	1.3.1 S	1.3.2 C	1.3.3 S	1.4.1 C	1.5.1 C	
	1.5.2 C	1.6.1 C	1.6.2 C	1.7.1 C	1.8.1 S	1.8.2 C	1.8.3 C		
	2.1.1 C	2.1.2 C	2.2.1 S	2.3.1 S	2.3.2 C	2.3.3 C	2.4.1 C	2.5.1 C	C9 S3
	2.5.2 C	2.6.1 C	2.6.2 C	2.7.1 C	2.8.1 S	2.8.2 C	2.8.3 C		
Lunge lesson Or Lead-rein lesson	3.1.1 C	3.2.1 C	3.2.2 S	3.3.1 C	3.4.1 C	3.5.1 C	3.6.1 C	3.7.1 C	
	3.7.2 C								
	4.1.1 C	4.1.2 S	4.2.1 C	4.3.1 C	4.4.1 C	4.5.1 C	4.6.1 C	4.7.1 C	C6 S1
	4.7.2 C								
Presentation	5.1.1 C	5.2.1 C	5.2.2 C	5.3.1 S	5.4.1 S	5.5.1 C	5.5.2 C		C3 S1
Business Knowledge/ Yard Organisation	6.1.1 C	6.1.2 C	6.1.3 S	6.1.4 C	6.1.5 C	6.2.1 S	6.2.2 S	6.3.1 C	C4 S2
	6.4.1 S	6.5.1 C							
Teaching Theory	7.1.1 S	7.2.1 C	7.3.1 C	7.4.1 C	7.5.1 C	7.5.2 C	7.6.1 C	7.6.2 S	C 11 S3
	7.7.1 C	7.8.1 S	7.9.1 S	7.10.1 C	7.11.1 C	7.11.2 C	7.12.1 C	7.12.2 C	
	7.13.1 C	7.13.2 C							
Duty of Care	8.1.1 C	8.2.1 S	8.2.2 S	8.3.1 C	8.4.1 C				C2 S1

The result sheet will be sent to you a few days after taking the exam and, if you have been successful, you will receive a certificate of achievement as well.

When you register for your PTT you will have the opportunity to also register for your United Kingdom Coaching Certificate (UKCC) Level 2 endorsement. The UKCC is a government initiative to introduce a standardised coaching qualification across all sports in the UK. Sportscoach UK (SCUK) is responsible for this, and the British Equestrian Federation (BEF) works with the SCUK to ensure its delivery across all the BEF member bodies. Equestrian Qualifications GB (the new name for the awarding body arm of the BHS) is responsible for awarding the qualification.

To achieve the BHS Generic UKCC Level 2 you will have to top up your PTT qualification by completing a portfolio.

The PTT Syllabus

Candidates must show that they have the required qualities, and can apply the basic principles of teaching, e.g. manner, voice, control, etc. and that they have the ability to improve their pupils' horsemanship and horsemastership using a progressive plan. They must know the safety procedures and principles involved in the organisation of a lesson or hack (in the open country or on roads). They will be required to give a class lesson, which may include poles/jumps, a lunge or lead-rein lesson, and a presentation.

Unit code number S3PTTE			
Learning Outcomes	**Element**	**Assessment criteria**	**Influence**
The candidate should be able to:		*The candidate has achieved this outcome because s/he can:*	
	1.1.1	Use his/her voice with good effect	Compulsory
Class Lesson on the flat	1.1.2	Display an appropriate manner enabling development of a rapport with pupils whilst maintaining control and facilitating learning	Compulsory
Show basic qualities needed in a riding instructor	1.2.1	Give a clear introduction outlining the format of the lesson	Supporting
Show methods and procedures used when assessing pupils	1.3.1	Use assessment exercises	Supporting
	1.3.2	Carry out procedures to maintain the ride's safety	Compulsory
	1.3.3	Discuss proposed lesson plan and lesson structure	Supporting
Produce a previously written lesson plan	1.4.1	Use appropriately planned exercises on the flat for improvement	Compulsory
Give a constructive class lesson to three or four riders	1.5.1	Identify riders' position strengths and weaknesses	Compulsory
	1.5.2	Give corrections to improve riders' position faults	Compulsory
	1.6.1	Identify aid application strengths and weaknesses	Compulsory
	1.6.2	Give corrections for aid application faults	Compulsory
Please refer to lesson topics 1-4	1.7.1	Select suitable school figures	Compulsory
	1.8.1	Give an action plan for future work	Supporting
TIME – 30 minutes	1.8.2	Obtain feedback from riders	Compulsory
	1.8.3	Self evaluate, reflect on performance, equipment and facilities	Compulsory
OR			
	2.1.1	Use his/her voice with good effect	Compulsory
Class Lesson using ground poles and jumps	2.1.2	Display an appropriate manner enabling development of a rapport with pupils whilst maintaining control and facilitating learning	Compulsory
Show basic qualities needed in a riding instructor	2.2.1	Give a clear introduction outlining the format of the lesson	Supporting
Show methods and procedures used when assessing pupils	2.3.1	Use assessment exercises	Supporting
	2.3.2	Carry out safe positioning of poles/fences and procedures to maintain the ride's safety	Compulsory
	2.3.3	Discuss proposed lesson plan and lesson structure	Supporting
Produce a previously written lesson plan	2.4.1	Use appropriately planned pole/jump exercises for improvement	Compulsory
Give a constructive class lesson to three or four riders	2.5.1	Identify riders' jumping strengths and weaknesses	Compulsory
	2.5.2	Give corrections to riders' jumping position faults	Compulsory
	2.6.1	Identify aid application strengths and weaknesses	Compulsory
	2.6.2	Give corrections for aid application faults	Compulsory
Please refer to lesson topics 5-8	2.7.1	Select suitable pole/jump distances	Compulsory
	2.8.1	Give an action plan for future work	Supporting
TIME – 30 minutes	2.8.2	Obtain feedback from riders	Compulsory
	2.8.3	Self evaluate, reflect on performance, equipment and facilities	Compulsory

It is important that the candidates work to involve the learners in the activities and build up a good rapport. Learners must be engaged and take an active part in the sessions. Candidates will also join in discussions and answer questions on various topics as detailed in the syllabus.

Unit code number S3PTTE			
Learning Outcomes	**Element**	**Assessment criteria**	**Influence**
The candidate should be able to:		*The candidate has achieved this outcome because s/he can:*	
Lunge lesson *Lesson topic:* Give a lunge lesson suitable for a beginner or novice rider. This may be to an adult or child Produce a previously written lesson plan TIME – 20 minutes	3.1.1	Assess horse and facilities and show appropriate handling of the horse/pony for a lunge lesson	Compulsory
	3.2.1	Assess the rider mounting and dismounting and their basic riding position needs	Compulsory
	3.2.2	Discuss proposed lesson plan and lesson structure	Supporting
	3.3.1	Choose work and exercises to bring about improvement in the rider's confidence, ability and position	Compulsory
	3.4.1	Show a lesson content that is lively, interesting and safe	Compulsory
	3.5.1	Develop a rapport with the rider through good communication	Compulsory
	3.6.1	Apply safe procedures throughout	Compulsory
	3.7.1	Obtain feedback from the rider and discuss future progression	Compulsory
	3.7.2	Self evaluate, reflect on performance, equipment and facilities	Compulsory
OR			
Lead-rein lesson *Lesson topic:* Give a lead rein lesson suitable for a beginner or novice rider. This may be to an adult or child Produce a previously written lesson plan TIME – 20 minutes	4.1.1	Assess facilities, the rider mounting, dismounting and their balance, security and position	Compulsory
	4.1.2	Discuss proposed lesson plan and lesson structure	Supporting
	4.2.1	Choose tasks and exercises appropriate for bringing about improvement in confidence, ability and position	Compulsory
	4.3.1	Show appreciation of the rider's age, previous experience and possible future progression	Compulsory
	4.4.1	Show a lesson content that is lively, interesting and safe	Compulsory
	4.5.1	Develop a rapport with the pupil through good communication	Compulsory
	4.6.1	Apply safe procedures throughout	Compulsory
	4.7.1	Obtain feedback from the rider	Compulsory
	4.7.2	Self evaluate, reflect on performance, equipment and facilities	Compulsory
Presentation Give a presentation of up to 10 minutes suitable for potential PTT candidates *Please refer to presentation topics 1-6*	5.1.1	Produce a logically planned presentation	Compulsory
	5.2.1	Deliver the presentation at the appropriate level and in a manner suitable to develop rapport and encourage learning	Compulsory
	5.2.2	Provide accurate presentation content at the appropriate level	Compulsory
	5.3.1	Use a range of explanation and demonstration techniques including props and visual aids as appropriate	Supporting
	5.4.1	Ensure learning has taken place	Supporting
	5.5.1	Obtain feedback from participants	Compulsory
	5.5.2	Self evaluate and reflect on performance	Compulsory
Business Knowledge / Yard Organisation Show knowledge of basic organisation of a commercial establishment	6.1.1	Outline procedures for receiving visitors	Compulsory
	6.1.2	List relevant information required from new clients	Compulsory
	6.1.3	List appropriate information given out to new clients, including assessment procedures	Supporting
	6.1.4	Describe the minimum clothing requirements for new clients	Compulsory
	6.1.5	Give examples of horse/rider allocation, including popular/unpopular horses	Compulsory
	6.2.1	Describe suitable methods of recording bookings and payments	Supporting
	6.2.2	Give examples of client retention schemes (money, hats, children's courses, etc.)	Supporting
	6.3.1	Describe procedures used to ensure new clients are assessed before joining a hack or ride	Compulsory
	6.4.1	Explain client numbers for group lessons and hacks	Supporting
	6.5.1	Describe how to look after riding surfaces and care for jump poles, wings, etc.	Compulsory

Unit code number S3PTTE			
Learning Outcomes	Element	Assessment criteria	Influence
The candidate should be able to:		*The candidate has achieved this outcome because s/he can:*	
	7.1.1	Outline the advantages and disadvantages of pupil grading systems	Supporting
	7.2.1	Describe how to brief assistants when giving a group lesson to lead rein riders	Compulsory
	7.3.1	Explain the advantages/disadvantages of private, class, lunge, lead-rein, horse-care lessons and hacks for pupils	Supporting
Teaching Theory	7.4.1	Describe an escort's responsibility for the ride with regard to control and safety on highways, open spaces and bridleways	Compulsory
Show a sound knowledge of basic equitation and be able to give clear explanations of lesson subjects and teaching format for the standard required for Stage 2 Riding	7.5.1	Give examples of factors which may lead to discomfort or distress in the horse or rider	Compulsory
	7.5.2	Give a description of a child rider experiencing too much physical effort and/or give the possible effects of demanding too much of adult riders	Compulsory
Evaluate the worth of different types of lessons	7.6.1	Outline the general format of a lesson	Compulsory
	7.6.2	Describe a logical progression of lessons from beginner to Stage 2 Riding on the flat and/or jumping	Supporting
Show an understanding of organising and escorting hacks	7.7.1	Give examples of when riders should hold:- the saddle, neck strap, reins	Compulsory
Show understanding of how rider fitness will impact on the lesson progress	7.8.1	Give examples of activities designed to make learning fun for children	Supporting
Show understanding of lesson structure and content	7.9.1	Describe how to teach new exercises	Supporting
	7.10.1	Describe and give examples of how to explain and teach the jumping position to riders	Compulsory
Show ability to assess rider progress	7.11.1	Explain the benefits of:- ground poles, placing poles, grids, related distances	Compulsory
Show knowledge of accident and emergency procedures	7.11.2	Give suitable distances for ground poles, placing poles, grids and related distances	Compulsory
	7.12.1	Discuss and/or give examples of how to motivate riders	Compulsory
	7.12.2	Give rules of use for indoor/outdoor arenas, schooling paddocks, jumps and cross country fences	Compulsory
	7.13.1	Discuss a safe procedure to be followed in case of an accident	Compulsory
	7.13.2	Outline the necessity for keeping records of accidents/incidents	Compulsory
	8.1.1	Explain the responsibilities imposed by 'duty of care'	Compulsory
Duty of Care	8.2.1	Describe good practice as it relates to teaching or supervising children	Supporting
Show a basic understanding and awareness of child protection issues and the way in which these matters may impact on teaching at this level.	8.2.2	Describe poor practice as it relates to teaching or supervising children	Supporting
	8.3.1	List indications of abuse	Compulsory
	8.4.1	Give appropriate action in response to child abuse. Take appropriate action In response to child abuse	Compulsory

PTT Syllabus 02–2008

They must have knowledge of how to proceed should there be an accident or an emergency and have sound knowledge of road safety.

N.B. Candidates may be required to give these lessons in the open and/or in a covered school. Ground poles or small jumps may be incorporated into the class lessons.

If you have recently taken Stage 1, 2 or 3, you will already be familiar with the new formatting of the syllabus, which now also applies to the PTT. For readers coming new to this system, it is clear and easy to follow. The syllabus is broken down into elements which are listed as either Compulsory or Supporting. Within this book the following symbols are used:

= C Compulsory

= S Supporting

You will be assessed on each of the main sections of the syllabus and to be successful you must achieve a minimum number of compulsory and supporting elements.

Study the syllabus carefully; the supporting elements are as important as the compulsory ones because they add strength and depth to your level of competence. Do not underestimate the value of the supporting elements – they help to reflect a sound level of competence in the candidate.

IMPORTANT: Candidates are advised to check that they are working from the latest examination syllabus, as examination content and procedure are liable to alteration. Contact the BHS Examinations Office for up-to-date information regarding the syllabus.

The Language of Equestrian Coaching

If you have been having regular instruction you will probably be aware of the terminology that is in general use for helping to keep the ride safe and under control. If you are coaching an individual with whom you have a good rapport and working relationship this terminology may appear too formal and unnecessary. It is very useful to be confident using the terminology because most riders will understand what is meant and, when working as a ride, will expect it.

- Working as a ride following each other is called working in closed order.

- Working as individuals within a group is called working in open order.

When asking all the riders to undertake an exercise together:

- 'Whole ride preparing to (e.g. go forward into working trot rising)'. Then pause to give the riders time to prepare themselves and their horses for the task. Then say 'Whole ride...trot'.

Example 2. (Asking the ride to undertake a figure when all are trotting)

- 'Whole ride twenty metre circle at A and then go large'.

When giving a command to undertake a task at a certain letter you must time the command so that the riders are able to prepare themselves and their horses and perform a smooth exercise.

When asking the riders to undertake an individual exercise with the rider in front going first the command 'Leading files in succession' is used. For example when asking each rider to canter one at a time to the rear of the ride:

- 'Leading files in succession prepare to go forward into working trot and at the next suitable corner pick up canter and canter to the rear of the ride'.

You should then ask the riders if they all understand what they have to do. You may point out the safety factors and that they must trot well before the rear file, or if they are unable to stop they should circle away. You then say 'Leading file commence the exercise'. Once they have finished you say 'Next commence' (or you could use their name which is more personal and friendly).

If you want the riders to undertake an exercise one at a time with the person at the rear going first you would use a similar sequence but use the term 'Rear files in succession...'

Always make sure commands are given in good enough time for the riders to prepare for whatever they are being asked to do. This will take practise. Listen to and watch experienced instructors/coaches to help understand how far in advance you need to prepare a group of riders to undertake an exercise successfully.

Rules of the School

It is important that you know the rules of the school and that the riders also understand those that are relevant to them.

The main rules are:

- Always knock and ask for permission to enter before going into a school or manége.

- When working as a ride always keep a safe distance from the horse in front.

- 'When working in open order:

  a) Always walk on an inner track, leaving the outer track free for those going at a faster pace.

  b) It is better to turn across the school to undertake a downwards transition so you do not interfere with horses behind you.

  c) Cross left hand to left hand with somebody working at the same pace as you.

  d) Give way to lateral work.

  e) Always be aware of what other riders are doing.

  f) Before leaving the school always inform other riders and ensure they have heard you.

Class Lesson on the Flat

The candidate should be able to:

Show basic qualities needed in a riding instructor.

Show methods and procedures used when assessing pupils.

Produce a previously written lesson plan.

Give a constructive class lesson to three or four riders.

ELEMENT

C	**1.1.1**	Use his/her voice with good effect.
C	**1.1.2**	Display an appropriate manner enabling development of a rapport with pupils whilst maintaining control and facilitating learning.
S	**1.2.1**	Give a clear introduction outlining the format of the lesson.
S	**1.3.1**	Use assessment exercises.
C	**1.3.2**	Carry out procedures to maintain the ride's safety.
S	**1.3.3**	Discuss proposed lesson plan and lesson structure.
C	**1.4.1**	Use appropriately planned exercises on the flat for improvement.
C	**1.5.1**	Identify riders' position strengths and weaknesses.
C	**1.5.2**	Give corrections to improve riders' position faults.
C	**1.6.1**	Identify aid application strengths and weaknesses.
C	**1.6.2**	Give corrections for aid application faults.
C	**1.7.1**	Select suitable school figures.
S	**1.8.1**	Give an action plan for future work.
C	**1.8.2**	Obtain feedback from riders.
C	**1.8.3**	Self-evaluate, reflect on performance, equipment and facilities.

What the assessor is looking for

- You should present a neat image with a clean, tidy, professional turnout, and from the outset you must convey confidence in both your voice and body language (Element 1.1.2).

- You should come with all your lesson plans prepared so you do not have to worry about these.

- Your voice must be positive and audible throughout the lesson (Element 1.1.1). Remember to project your voice with clear words that are not hurried. Position the ride near to the assessor when you are talking to your pupils, so that the assessor can hear too.

- It is likely that your riders will be mounted and waiting for you in a line. Introduce yourself and find out your riders' names and check their tack (Element 1.2.1). Ask your riders if there is anything specific they would like to work on as individuals. Also ask if they need help with either their reins or stirrups and suggest they check their girths. Find out if the riders are all mounted on horses they have ridden before (Element 1.3.1).

- Discuss what you have been asked to teach, so that your pupils know the subject matter or aims of the lesson that you will give (Element 1.2.1).

Correct riding position – shoulder, hip and heel aligned.

A typical novice rider position, as yet showing no depth.

Rider faults: rounded shoulders, stiff arms, over-short reins, rounded back.

Rider faults: sitting behind the movement, reins too long, and lower leg forward.

- Demonstrate confidence and ability in your control of the ride as you start to work with them (Element 1.1.2). It does not matter if you choose to work the ride in closed order or in open order so long as you have clearly directed the ride in what they are to do and you are sure that they both understand and can carry out your instructions.

- Choose work that shows you know how to assess riders and progress the work to a logical plan (Elements 1.3.2, 1.4.1 and 1.7.1).

- Be able to identify where riders have faults and weaknesses and be able to offer assistance for improvement (Elements 1.5.1 and 1.6.1).

- Once you have assessed the riders the assessor will discuss with you how you feel the lesson will progress and whether the lesson plan needs to be adapted.

- Show confidence in choosing work that will address the riders' faults and help to improve them (Elements 1.5.2 and 1.6.2).

- Choose school figures that help to develop the riders' competence and feel for the horses, from which you can make suitable corrections of position faults or aid application (Element 1.7.1).

- Frequently encourage the riders to feed back to you by asking them questions that will make them think about what they are doing (Element 1.8.2).

- At the end of the lesson be confident about talking to the group as a whole (briefly) and then individually. Provide some clear ideas for further improvement by giving the riders something to be working on in the coming days or weeks after the lesson (Element 1.8.1).

- The assessor will then discuss the lesson and riders with you. You should reflect on the lesson truthfully, pointing out what went well, what could have gone better and how you could have improved it. The assessor will discuss this with you. He/she will also obtain feedback from the riders.

How to become competent

- You will be required to teach a group of three riders for between 30 and 35 minutes. The riders should be able to walk, trot and canter and jump small fences. The lesson will probably take place in a 20m x 40m school which may be indoors or outside.

- Practise remembering names, as it is important to be involved with your riders and forgetting their names does not promote this feeling. If you find it difficult to remember names then take a small notebook or postcard with you to jot down names so that a glance down will remind you (e.g. Sarah – bay horse with martingale; John – brown horse, white brushing boots).

- With any riders for whom you are responsible, remind them to check their girths before you move off and again after five or ten minutes' riding. Be able to adjust stirrups for your riders and/or advise on level stirrups.

- It is important for safety reasons to ask the riders if they have ridden the horse before, have they checked their girths and stirrups?

- An initial assessment of the group is vital (it allows you to decide how the work should progress). This assessment might involve some walk, trot and canter with a change of direction.

- During this assessment, while maybe not yet fully 'teaching' your pupils, nevertheless you should communicate with them, beginning to introduce some strengths and weaknesses in the riders. It is acceptable to work the ride in closed or open order as long as you explain clearly which you are choosing and why. If

VARIOUS WAYS TO CHANGE THE REIN

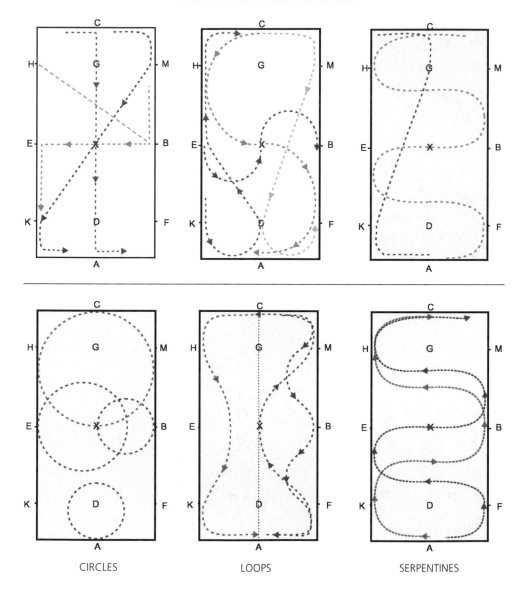

CIRCLES LOOPS SERPENTINES

As a coach, you have a vast number of school figures to choose from when planning exercises. Know them well, and, as important, know how to teach them accurately.

you choose open order you must check the riders are used to this and understand the rules of the school.

- With fairly inexperienced riders it is often easier to assess them in closed order rather than have fairly novice riders you have never taught before in open order.

- In the first few minutes learn to assess the basic competence and control of each rider, the basic position, whether they are 'leaders' or 'followers'.

- Choose simple straightforward exercises to start with, going large, 20m circles and changes of rein across the diagonal.

- You must be able to assess each rider's correct basic position and to decide, if there are faults, from where they originate. (E.g. a loose position may be caused by the rider trying to ride with overlong stirrups. Heels drawing up may be caused by the rider gripping with the lower leg and thus drawing the heel up.)

- Watch as many class lessons as you can so that you see riders' positions and faults and what other instructors do to improve them.

- Understand the value of working riders without stirrups (in walk, trot and/or canter) to develop the depth and effect of the rider's position.

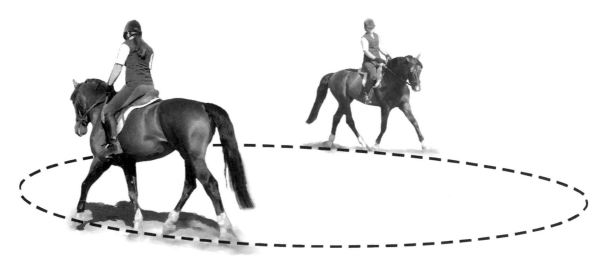

Riding a circle. Teach your riders the aids that create this figure: inside rein indicating direction; inside leg on the girth for energy, motivating the inside hind leg; outside rein controlling the pace and bend; and outside leg controlling the hindquarters, slightly behind the girth.

- Choose work that will not overtire your riders or be beyond their ability, which then may cause a loss of confidence and compromise safety.

- You must talk to your riders to find out their knowledge and obtain feedback to fully understand what they are feeling and thinking.

- It is important that the riders understand the aids for basic exercises (e.g. turns, circles, simple changes of pace and direction).

- It is your responsibility to maintain safety in the lesson at all times and to the best of your ability. You must therefore make clear judgements about what to do and when to do it. This is always dependent on the circumstances 'on that day'.

- Always teach what you see in front of you and what is actually happening. Never teach a lesson that you think the assessor might want to see, or that the rider chooses, despite your being doubtful about the rider's competence.

- Development of the work is essential for maintaining enthusiasm and motivating riders towards further achievement.

- Repetition is essential for ensuring that your riders become competent.

- By watching other instructors you will develop a range of exercises, movements and work that will provide the repetition for riders, while also introducing variety to maintain interest.

- As a preliminary teacher **never** assume knowledge. Even if a rider tells you that he or she can canter or jump you must always make your own assessment and progress the work in accordance with **your** judgement.

- **Never** pressurise a rider into attempting to do something that they tell you they cannot or do not want to do.

- **Always** have your full attention on your rider(s). Do not be distracted by anything or anyone who disturbs the lesson.

- Whenever possible, riders should be of similar standard in a lesson. Progress should be directed by the least competent rider in the group.

- Learn to be aware of outside influences which might have a disrupting effect on your class lesson (e.g. horses turned out in a field, galloping about / noisy vehicle outside the school). Awareness can allow you to adapt the lesson content (e.g. come back to walk if working in trot or canter) so that safety is maintained before control is lost.

- Make sure that you understand the basis of the rider being able to ride the horse forward from leg to hand and that the security of the rider's position dictates their ability to apply clear and coordinated aids.

- Practise projecting your voice with confidence throughout the lesson. Clearly expressed words can then be easily heard and will not be lost into the surface or into the wind if outside.

Class Lesson Using Ground Poles and Jumps

Show basic qualities needed in a riding instructor.

Show methods and procedures used when assessing pupils.

Produce a previously written lesson plan.

Give a constructive class lesson to three or four riders.

ELEMENT

C	**2.1.1**	Use his/her voice with good effect.
C	**2.1.2**	Display an appropriate manner enabling development of a rapport with pupils whilst maintaining control and facilitating learning.
S	**2.2.1**	Give a clear introduction outlining the format of the lesson.
S	**2.3.1**	Use assessment exercises.
C	**2.3.2**	Carry out safe positioning of poles/fences and procedures to maintain the ride's safety.
S	**2.3.3**	Discuss proposed lesson plan and lesson structure.
C	**2.4.1**	Use appropriately planned pole/jump exercises for improvement.
C	**2.5.1**	Identify riders' jumping strengths and weaknesses.
C	**2.5.2**	Give corrections to riders' jumping position faults.
C	**2.6.1**	Identify aid application strengths and weaknesses.
C	**2.6.2**	Give corrections for aid application faults.
C	**2.7.1**	Select suitable pole/jump distances.
S	**2.8.1**	Give an action plan for future work.

C **2.8.2** Obtain feedback from riders.

C **2.8.3** Self-evaluate, reflect on performance, equipment and facilities.

What the assessor is looking for

- The Elements 2.1.1, 2.1.2, 2.2.1 and 2.3.1. are identical to those in Element 1 for the class lesson on the flat, so it is important that you read carefully the information relating to Elements 1.1.1, 1.1.2, 1.2.1 and 1.3.1.

- Come to the exam with your lesson plans prepared so you do not have to worry about these on the day.

- With a jumping lesson, the handling of the equipment that you need (poles, jump wings, cups, etc.) must be done with proficiency and competence, through familiarity and awareness of where to place the equipment with regard to maintaining the safety of your ride (Element 2.3.2).

- Ideally, in an exam you will have someone to assist you so that the equipment can be moved into place for you to use without reducing your valuable teaching time.

- You must inform your helper where the poles/jumps are to be placed and you must **always check yourself** that the jump and any distances have been placed or measured to your satisfaction.

- Spare equipment should be stacked neatly out of the way of the ride's activity, with special awareness of keeping jump cups tidy and safe. Jump cups must never be left on a wing if they are not holding a pole.

- You must assess the ride with particular emphasis on the lesson being a jumping lesson (Element 2.3.1). It would therefore be wise to ensure that the riders are **riding with stirrups at jumping length** before you start. Probably see them in walk, trot and canter and ask them to take 'light seat' at some stage of this initial work.

- Once you have assessed the ride the assessor will discuss with you how you feel the lesson will progress and whether the lesson plan will be adapted.

- You must be able to recognise when the rider is in good balance in the jumping position (Element 2.5.1).

- You must also be able to identify the area(s) of fault with the riders' positions and be able to suggest help to assist in improvement (Element 2.5.2).

- You must be able to recognise if faults are arising from poor balance or incorrect position, or from poor understanding of the use of correct aids or their application (Element 2.6.1).

- If aid application is the problem, then relevant help must be forthcoming once you have identified the weak area (Element 2.6.2).

- Your choice of work will be directed by your initial assessment and also to some degree by the 'brief' you are given for your lesson. The 'brief' is a broad-based subject around which you should be structuring your lesson plan. For example, if your brief was to use poles for balance of the rider then you would use only poles. If your lesson were to involve one or two fences with a change of direction, then your plan would be different and include jumps.

- Whatever you choose for your lesson, you must use appropriate distances between your poles and safely constructed jumps according to the ability of your horses and riders (Element 2.7.1).

Rider showing a 'light seat' or jumping position
(also known as forward seat or poised position).

- At the end of the lesson be confident to talk to the group as a whole (briefly) and then individually. Discuss each rider's strengths and weaknesses and give them an idea of points to work on for the future.

The assessor will then discuss the lesson and riders with you. You should reflect on the lesson truthfully, pointing out what went well, what could have gone better and how you could have improved it. The assessor will discuss this with you. He/she will also obtain feedback from the riders.

How to become competent

- For any lesson of any level you must be confident, and confidence only comes from experience and feeling comfortable and familiar with what you are doing.

- Watch as many jumping lessons as you can, given by more experienced instructors.

- Go to jumping competitions and watch riders competing.

Working in jumping position over a single pole and several poles.

- Become very familiar with how jumps are built, from a simple cross pole to a more demanding double on one or two non-jumping strides, to a vertical fence and an oxer.

- Help more experienced jumping teachers while they teach, but be in the school and help them move fences and put down poles, so that you develop an awareness of how quickly and efficiently you must learn to use the equipment.

- Learn to keep your eyes constantly on your riders; even if you are moving poles with your feet, or adjusting the height of a fence, you must keep watching your riders.

- **Never** allow a rider to approach a fence if you do not have your eyes on them – and preferably your full attention as well.

- Occasionally, you may still be speaking to a rider who has just completed an exercise but you **must** be looking at the rider who is starting to negotiate the fence or poles.

- In the early stages of your teaching you may need to have only one rider moving around at a time so you do not have too much to concentrate on. As you develop in competence it is acceptable and practical to have the riders working in open order and working over poles using their judgement to maintain space from each other.

- Awareness is vital, you must be able to develop a 'feel' for when a horse is getting a little sharp and may start to rush a jump, or when a rider is getting nervous and starting to 'hold back' restricting the forwardness to a jump.

- Watch more senior instructors working with different riders through grids and jumping exercises.

- You must learn basic distances for jumping but ultimately it is how you 'teach' the rider that dictates whether the distance works for that horse or rider or not.

- Take basic distances such as: trotting pole distance at 4ft 6in (1.35m) apart; a placing pole to a small fence taken from trot at approx 9ft (2.7m); a trot approach to a small fence followed by one non-jumping stride to a second fence on 18ft (5.4m); and the same two fences with a canter approach 21ft (6.3m). These distances would be acceptable for a basic jumping lesson with rhythmical reasonable forward paces. However, the teacher must be able to help adjust the approach if necessary if a distance is riding too long or short, rather than just identifying the distance as being 'wrong'.

- A basic ability to 'see' whether a distance suits a horse and rider or not is essential at this level. This must be learned through 'feel', awareness and discussion with a more senior instructor who will help you to see what they are seeing and aware of.

- You must teach some basic jumping lessons, use poles regularly and feel familiar with moving poles around and recognising when the poles have been rolled out of place.

- Learn to work in a tidy safe environment and always move spare poles into a tidy stack out of the way of the working ride.

- **Always** take cups out of stands if they are not holding a pole.

- Always keep spare cups tucked under the sides of wings or in the spare stack of jumps or in a designated receptacle.

- Collapsable cups should be used for the back rail of a spread fence.

- If in doubt always check a distance if you think it has been moved or is inappropriate, telling a rider to wait before approaching a fence.

- Always choose exercises and fences that are well within the range of ability of your riders.

- Be able to discuss what future work you might do with riders on another occasion. Never rush to build an extra fence or another element to a grid when that might compromise safety. Discuss the option of putting in another fence or part to a grid as a possibility for a future lesson.

- Be prepared to talk truthfully about how the lesson went, and to give your thoughts and feelings about it. Reflecting on what you have done is important. If you are unable to realise what has gone well and what has not, then it is difficult for you to improve your coaching methods. Remember, nobody is perfect and we can always improve by approaching something a different way, or by spotting problems earlier, or by choosing different exercises to help riders.

Lunge Lesson

Give a lunge lesson suitable for a beginner or novice rider. This may be to an adult or a child.

Produce a previously written lesson plan.

Time – 25 minutes.

ELEMENT

| C | **3.1.1** Assess horse and facilities and show appropriate handling of the horse/pony for a lunge lesson. |

3.1.1 Assess horse and facilities and show appropriate handling of the horse/pony for a lunge lesson.

3.2.1 Assess the rider mounting and dismounting and their basic riding position needs.

3.2.2 Discuss proposed lesson plan and lesson structure.

3.3.1 Choose work and exercises to bring about improvement in the rider's confidence, ability and position.

3.4.1 Show a lesson content that is lively, interesting and safe.

3.5.1 Develop a rapport with the rider through good communication.

3.6.1 Apply safe procedures throughout.

3.7.1 Obtain feedback from the rider and discuss future progression.

3.7.2 Self-evaluate, reflect on performance, equipment and facilities.

- The lunge lesson lasts 25 minutes in total. You will be given a brief that is relevant to the rider you are given. It will probably involve asking you to assess the rider and work to improve their position. The rider may be a child or an adult, and they should be of a beginner/novice standard.

- Come to the exam with a generic lesson plan which you will be able to adapt on the day.

- You should introduce yourself to the rider and ask them their name and to tell you how much riding they have done. Ask them if they have any particular issues they would like to work on and what their long-term goals are. Then ask them to stand in a safe place within the school (possibly a corner, or if the school is divided by poles, then outside the pole area).

- The horse will have been warmed up for you so it will be necessary only to ensure that he is responsive to your aids. Briefly check the tack and if you have any issues discuss these with your assessor. Send the horse out onto one rein (most people send the horse out onto the left rein first, so this may be advisable as he may be expecting that). Lunge him for a few circles asking for one or two trot/walk/trot transitions. Be positive so that you quickly take command of the situation. Do not forget your rider in the corner – if this were a real lesson they would be paying for your time. Perhaps discuss the number of beats in walk and trot with them or talk about the benefits of lungeing. Change the rein, attach the side-reins and try the horse briefly on the other rein. If you feel there are any issues with regard to using this horse for a novice lunge lesson then talk to the assessor about it. This assessment should take no more than a few minutes.

- Stop the horse, unclip the side reins, untwist the reins, check the girth and then mount your rider. Make sure that the rider uses a correct technique for mounting. They can mount from a mounting block if you feel that is advisable. Remember, mounting from a block is easier for the horse as well as the rider. Ensure that the rider checks the stirrup length before they mount and, although you must check the girth, encourage them to get into the habit of also checking it themselves. When your rider mounts, assist as necessary and check their technique. See that they have turned the stirrup the right way and that the reins are correctly held. During all this you must have control of the horse, and your whip should be safely tucked under your arm with the lash end of the whip pointing towards the ground and the lash behind you.

- Once the rider is mounted check that their stirrups are level and do not forget to attach the horse's side-reins. Assess the rider briefly on both reins and decide where their positional issues lie. (Element 3.2.1)

Stirrup leathers snugly and securely crossed over the withers so that the rider can work comfortably without stirrups.

Lungeing the rider without stirrups to improve position, depth and security.

- You will then have an opportunity to discuss your proposed lesson plan with the assessor. (Element 3.2.2) Be honest about your rider and tell the assessor what you feel about their position, confidence and ability and put forward your ideas as to what you are going to do. Remember the rider will hear this, so be polite about them and always say something positive first.

- The main body of the lesson is working to improve the rider. (Element 3.3.1) The exercises you choose must be relevant to the rider's issues. It is no use giving arm-circling exercises when the rider is very stiff in the hips. A lot of beginner and novice riders are very tight through their hips. This can be partly due to nerves and partly due to general stiffness through the joints. Always work to get the rider central in the saddle with the two imaginary straight lines running ear–shoulder–hip–heel and elbow–arm–reins–bit rings.

- Your rider may well need to hold the neck strap or pommel to help maintain their balance. This should be encouraged. They will feel safer and then relax into their position more.

- A rider who sits in an armchair position needs to be encouraged to sit up. Riding briefly with one hand in the small of the back will help to give them the feel of sitting on their seat bones. Holding a hand in that position can be very tiring (as can any exercise that the rider is not used to) so make sure you do not overstress the rider. Standing in the stirrups (holding the neck strap at halt in the first instance) can also encourage an armchair rider to come more into balance. A rider who is very behind the movement may well have their stirrups too short. Riding without stirrups is excellent to help lengthen the rider's legs and generally improve balance and position. You must assess whether you think the rider is secure enough to ride without stirrups.

- There is no set rule as to whether or not you take away the reins or stirrups from the rider. You must assess whether doing either will help the rider to improve. When coaching in a known environment with a known client you may well take away the reins and stirrups at the same time. However, in an exam situation, with a rider and a horse you do not know, it may be advisable to take away just one thing at a time if you feel doing so could benefit the rider.

- During the session it is important to keep your rider involved. (Element 3.4.1) Ask frequently for feedback about how what they are doing feels and if they can feel any difference in their position. (Element 3.5.1) Depending on the experience of the rider you can also ask them about the feel they are getting from the horse itself. Do not just bark orders at them all the time. Ask them about how their body feels and how tired it is becoming. Allow them time to give you feedback and make sure you react to it. (Element 3.7.1)

- At the end of the session bring the horse to a halt, walk to the horse and undo the side-reins. Talk to the rider about their strengths and weaknesses and give them some things to work on during their next session. Dismount the rider safely and make sure they run up their stirrups.

- The assessor will then approach you to discuss the session. (Element 3.7.2) Think carefully about what has happened and identify the positives. If you feel there is anything that could have been undertaken differently then discuss this also. Self-reflection is an important part of coaching – unless we think about what we have done and how we have done it, it will be very difficult to improve ourselves.

- The assessor will ask the rider (Element 3.7.1) to give very briefly one or two thoughts on the session. As long as you have built up a good rapport, involved the rider and used exercises that are relevant you should not worry about this at all.

- Many coaches seem to spend a great deal of time making the rider undertake arm- and leg-circling exercises. If these are relevant to the rider's issues then you will not be penalised, but if they are just being used to 'fill up' the lesson time you will be marked down.

- There are many useful exercises you can use to help improve a rider's position (see next section). In an exam it is always best to ask the rider to undertake any exercises initially at halt. This will be easier for them and you can assess the reaction of the horse.

- It is absolutely vital that you pay attention to safety throughout the session. It is no easy task to control a horse and give a lunge lesson at the same time. Your lungeing technique must be efficient and effective. It is possible to fail this section if you are not safe. A rider will not have confidence in you as a coach if you are inefficient and give the impression of uncertainty.

What the assessor is looking for

- The first thing the assessor will be looking for is a safe and established lungeing technique; without this you will be unable to give a competent lesson (Element 3.1.1).

- Ensure that you are well practised in lungeing and you feel confident in lungeing unknown horses.

- It is essential that you are able to send the horse forward sufficiently in order to give a competent lesson.

- Mount the rider **with the side-reins unclipped from the bit**, clip up the side-reins and work the rider first with the reins and stirrups while you make an initial assessment (Element 3.2.1).

- In this assessment, the assessor will want to see you make clear observations about the rider's position, noticing both the strengths and weaknesses.

- The lesson should be active and interesting (Element 3.4.1). Be sure to make frequent changes of rein and work in an animated way with your pupil, making sure they are kept involved. (Element 3.5.1).

- Throughout the whole lesson you must demonstrate safety and awareness (Element 3.6.1).

How to become competent

- I make no apology for repeating that there are no short cuts to competence. You must practise lungeing frequently and with as many different horses as possible.

- **Your lungeing technique must be secure and consistent**. Make sure that you can manage the rein and whip efficiently on both reins, without getting the rein muddled.

- Make sure that you have lunged a rider as often as possible; if you can, start with a pony (and child) which tends to be easier to manage, and then move to a horse and adult rider.

- Watch more experienced instructors giving lunge lessons and try to have a lesson or two yourself.

- Practise exercises that might be useful to improve riders, feel the effect they have on your position and consider the value they have.

- Gradually develop a range of exercises which work different parts of the body and help the rider's balance and suppleness.

  Suggested exercises for improving the softness of the hips and lower body:

  • Asking the rider to bring their whole leg back from the hip.

  • Lifting up the knees, turning them out and pushing legs down and back.

  • With the hand hold the foot and draw the lower leg up so the leg is near to the cantle.

  • Ankle circling.

  • Standing up in the stirrups.

Suggested exercises for improving the softness of the upper body:

• Put chin to chest and then tilt the head back.

• Shoulder Shrugs.

• Shoulder rolls.

• Turn head to look as far left as possible and then as far right as possible.

• Rotate the upper body left then right.

■ Learn to lunge a horse briefly and then mount a rider quickly and efficiently so that you do not waste time in this process and can get on with your lesson.

■ Time is always limited in an exam and the more proficient you can be in getting on with any lesson, the more experience you will demonstrate and the more time you will have to improve your pupil.

■ Your safety and awareness is paramount. If in doubt about how a horse might be behaving or reacting then be cautious before taking away reins or stirrups. If a horse is misbehaving at the other end of the school and your rider is without stirrups, give them back their stirrups as a precautionary measure and say why you are doing that.

■ Show an ability to communicate with your pupils; knowing how they feel about the work you are doing, will help in their learning process.

■ Your awareness of the **correct basic riding position** is always of prime importance. Make sure that you can recognise when a rider is sitting correctly or where they are out of balance and need help to adjust their position.

■ Watch many riders and their positions and their balance and how this may change according to what they are trying to do with the horse or how the horse is going.

Lead-Rein Lesson

Give a lead-rein lesson suitable for a beginner or novice rider. This may be to an adult or child.

Produce a previously written lesson plan.

Time – 25 minutes.

ELEMENT

| C | **4.1.1** Assess facilities, the rider mounting, dismounting and their balance, security and position. |

4.1.1 Assess facilities, the rider mounting, dismounting and their balance, security and position.

4.1.2 Discuss proposed lesson plan and lesson structure.

4.2.1 Choose tasks and exercises appropriate for bringing about improvement in confidence, ability and position.

4.3.1 Show appreciation of the rider's age, previous experience and possible future progression.

4.4.1 Show a lesson content that is lively, interesting and safe.

4.5.1 Develop a rapport with the pupil through good communication.

4.6.1 Apply safe procedures throughout.

4.7.1 Obtain feedback from the rider.

4.7.2 Self-evaluate, reflect on performance, equipment and facilities.

- You will give either a lunge or a lead-rein lesson.

- The lead-rein lesson will last 25 minutes in total. You will be given a brief that is relevant to the rider you have. It will probably involve assessing the rider and working to improve their position. The rider will either be a child or a beginner adult.

- Many people think that a lead-rein lesson is a 'soft option'. To give a good lead-rein lesson, however, is extremely difficult. To position yourself so you can build up a rapport with the rider, control the horse/pony and give a worthwhile lesson takes a great deal of practice. You need to be by the horse/pony's shoulder. You should not be in front of the horse/pony and 'drag' it along. You need to be able to look at the rider when you are talking to them to build up a rapport and ensure that what they are doing is correct, but you must also be aware of where you are going!

- Introduce yourself to the rider, ask their name and spend a short time talking to them to start to build up a rapport. Discuss what riding they have done and what their goals are. Ask them if they have ridden the horse/pony before and, if they have, what he is like. Check the tack. Make sure there is a neck strap and that the method given to you to lead the horse is safe.

- If the rider is a complete beginner you will have to teach them to mount. Make sure you are accurate in this. If they can ride a little then ensure they mount correctly. Using a mounting block is a good idea. It makes the task easier for both horse and rider. Pay particular attention to checking the girth and stirrup length before mounting. Try to get the rider into good habits right from the beginning by ensuring the reins and stirrups are not twisted and that the rider understands the horse has feelings.

- Once the rider is mounted make sure you check that the stirrups are of an equal length and they are sitting centrally.

- Spend a few minutes assessing the rider. Work on both reins and at the same time make sure you are taking responsibility for the control of the horse/pony. Decide on what the rider's issues are and how you can go about improving them. Then spend a few minutes discussing with the assessor what you are going to do and why. (Element 4.1.2) Remember: you will be in ear- shot of the rider, so be polite about them and point out the positives first.

- The main part of your lesson is how you work the rider to improve them. It is important that the exercises you use take the rider's age and previous experience into consideration (Element 4.3.1). The exercises must be relevant to the rider. Safety must be the priority (Element 4.6.1), but the lesson must be interesting and lively as well (Element 4.4.1). If the rider is a complete beginner they may need to hold the neck strap or pommel for most of the work at the beginning of the session. Do not overface the rider with the exercises you choose. Children may well enjoy toe touching exercises at the halt, helping to make a weak lower leg secure, but a beginner adult may find this exercise difficult, and that does nothing to boost their confidence.

- If the rider is a complete beginner you may find yourself staying in walk the whole lesson. You may progress to a small amount of sitting trot. It is vital that you ask the rider to undertake work that will help to build confidence and competence and not just 'use up' the lesson time. If you feel it is relevant and safe to do so, you can do work without stirrups. Take time to engage the rider in conversation – a rider who is talking is breathing and therefore less stiff than one who is holding their breath. Get them to think about what they are doing and to tell you how it feels. All this will help with building a rapport (Element 4.5.1) and will ensure the rider enjoys themself as well as learns. It is vital that a child's lesson is fun, but that does not mean to say you should sacrifice their position or ability to improve for this.

- Change the rein frequently. There may well be another lead-rein lesson going on in the same area. Keep an eye out for what the other combination is doing so you do not get in each other's way. The assessor may well be moving around the area with you. They will not get in the way. They are just ensuring they hear what is being said, giving you every opportunity to show your abilities.

- If you feel the rider is competent in walk and trot you may wish to let them off the lead rein. It may be best at first to walk and trot them while you are holding the very end of the lead rein a short distance away from them, just to make sure they can cope. If you do let them off the lead rein, stay close to them.

- If there is time you may wish to use cones/blocks or poles for the rider to negotiate as an obstacle course. Even riding around a single cone can give a beginner rider a real challenge and create much discussion.

- Remember to be enthusiastic and show a real desire to keep your rider motivated. Whenever you teach you must really want your riders to improve, and this is just as true for a lead-rein lesson as for a class session.

- At the end of the session the assessor will give you an opportunity to reflect on the lesson. Be honest with yourself and the assessor. Do find the positives from the session, and if you feel there was anything you could have done differently then discuss it. (Element 4.7.2) The assessor may well question you on specific areas or engage in a general discussion about what they have seen. They will also briefly ask the rider for feedback on the session. (Element 4.7.1)

What the assessor is looking for

- It is essential with any novice or beginner rider that you are able to assess the person's basic balance when they first get onto the horse/pony. Some riders have a greater natural balance, confidence and ability to sit automatically in the optimum position on a horse than others. The naturally balanced, confident rider will tend to find more security from the start. You must show an ability to recognise the beginner or novice rider's innate ability (Element 4.1.1).

- Be able to work out if the rider is insecure or unbalanced and know how to make adjustments which will help them adopt a more correct balanced position (Element 4.2.1).

- You must show an ability to develop a good rapport with the rider, being tactful and encouraging. The rider must be involved. (Element 4.5.1).

- The age of the rider may be relevant to their level of confidence and understanding and to their attention span and this should be a consideration shown in the way you teach (Element 4.3.1).

- The lesson must demonstrate safe practice at all time and should show a progression which is interesting and appropriate for the confidence and level of ability of the rider (Elements 4.3.1 and 4.4.1).

How to become competent

- If you can gain some genuine experience of giving lead-rein lessons or assisting in leading while another instructor is teaching, then this will be invaluable to you.

- Watch novice and beginner riders being taught by someone of more experience.

- Watch the inadequacies that the majority of beginners have when their only contact with the horse/pony may be for one hour per week.

- Remember that someone who is able to practise a skill daily or even several times a week will be much more proficient than someone who has only one hour each week to revisit their chosen activity.

- You must be constantly aware of the need to assist and repeat terms and actions which to you may be very familiar but to the novice or beginner rider are still quite alien.

- Be aware that it takes many repetitions of simple tasks to achieve even a basic level of competence, so do not worry that you may appear to be repeating things many times over.

- Try to develop a versatility in repeating the same task or information without confusing your rider. In this way you will keep lessons interesting while ensuring that sufficient repetition does convey competence gradually (e.g. In walk there are many changes of rein that could be used to encourage your rider to concentrate on the aids for turning).

- Make sure that you are competent in leading both ponies (for child riders) and horses (for adults) working evenly on both reins and being able to lead the animal efficiently, especially in trot, while still able to glance at your rider and make simple suggestions.

- You need to be physically fit enough to conduct a twenty- to thirty-minute lesson on foot involving walk and trot and capably communicating with your pupil without getting breathless.

- If you are sharing the school with other lessons going on simultaneously make sure you use the school sensibly and with awareness of other instructors.

Presentation

The candidate should be able to:

Give a presentation of up to 10 minutes suitable for potential PTT candidates.

ELEMENT

- C **5.1.1** Produce a logically planned presentation.

- C **5.2.1** Deliver the presentation at the appropriate level and in a manner suitable to develop rapport and encourage learning.

- C **5.2.2** Provide accurate presentation content at the appropriate level.

- S **5.3.1** Use a range of explanation and demonstration techniques including props and visual aids as appropriate.

- S **5.4.1** Ensure learning has taken place.

- C **5.5.1** Obtain feedback from participants.

- C **5.5.2** Self-evaluate and reflect on performance.

General guidelines on presentations

People learn best when they are actively involved with the learning process, this helps their understanding and improves their interest and motivation to learn. It also allows them to build on their experience and relate information to prior knowledge and understanding.

With this in mind the classroom teaching section should reflect the above principles. Candidates are encouraged to move away from didactic (chalk and talk) approaches to this section. Instead the candidate should involve the group in an interactive, discussion style presentation. The use of visual aids should be used to facilitate this, through the use of a white/blackboard or flip chart.

Candidates are encouraged to use questions and answers to discover the group's prior subject knowledge. This information could be used to form the base for a discussion.

Lesson plans on each subject area should be prepared beforehand. These must be included in the portfolio. Lesson plans should be kept simple and allow the candidate to relate subject information to the groups prior knowledge of the subject area.

Each candidate is allocated up to ten minutes. It is important that candidates are realistic about how much content can be covered in this time and think carefully about time allocation when preparing their lesson plan. It is not necessary to use the whole 10 minutes to prove to assessors that candidates are up to standard in this section.

Below is an **example of a lesson plan**, which can be adapted for each subject area.

Subject: Goal setting and why it is important

Resources required: White board and pens

Duration of lesson: Up to 10 minutes

Timing: Activity/content

0–2   Introduction to subject area and its importance.

2–4   Use questions to find out groups understanding of the benefits of goal setting.

4–8   Discuss the use of short, interim and long term goal setting.

8–9   Ask group if they have any questions and give appropriate answers.

9–10   Conclude subject.

Self evaluation

The following pages provide example content for various presentations. The information is not prescriptive nor comprehensive, and should not be copied 'word for word'. The bullet points suggest further key points that are suitable for inclusion. Candidates are encouraged to choose one of the key points for further discussion.

1. Goal setting and why it is important

Goal setting assists the coach in improving and monitoring a rider's performance.

It is suggested that any of the following subjects are suitable for inclusion within the discussion on goal setting;-

- The use of the acronym SMART. Goals should be SPECIFIC to the individual or group. MEASURABLE, ACHIEVABLE, REALISTIC and given a TIMEFRAME.

- How goal setting can increase riders pride and satisfaction in their performance.

- The advantages of using performance based rather than outcome related goals, thereby measuring improvement in the rider's personal best, rather than relating goals to winning a competition.

- The use of goal setting in improving and maintaining a rider's motivation.

- How the coach can actively involve riders in setting goals in order to ensure their needs and aspirations are met.

- The use of short, interim and long term goal setting.

- Matching goals to the strengths and weaknesses of riders.

- How goal setting can improve the quality of your training sessions.

- The need to regularly review goals and adapt or change them if necessary.

- How goal setting can be used to improve a riders self confidence.

2. The importance of warm-up and cool-down for riders and horses

It is essential to warm up horses and riders to ensure that they are mentally and physically ready to commence and gain maximum benefit from a training session.

Correct warming-up techniques increase blood flow around the body, increasing the riders' and horses' flexibility and help to prevent injuries by increasing circulation and body temperature. Stretching will help prepare muscles for work and make them less prone to wear and tear. It is important to stretch each of the main muscle groups in the warm up and include light aerobic activity.

Effective cooling-off, using light aerobic activity and gentle stretches, will help to prevent muscle stiffness and aid recovery, ensuring that both horse and rider are mentally and physically ready to return to pre-training activities. It also helps the body dispose of waste products that have built up whilst exercising.

It is suggested that the following subjects are suitable for inclusion in a lesson discussing the importance of warm-up and cool-down for riders and horses:

- The safety considerations of warming up horses that are over enthusiastic or 'fresh.'

- Safety considerations that relate to warming up novice or beginner riders.

- The use of un-mounted warm up exercises.

- Suitable exercises for warming up and cooling down riders and horses.

- How to recognise when a rider or horse has warmed up sufficiently to begin training.

- How to recognise when a rider or horse has cooled down sufficiently to conclude a training session.

- The use of stretching exercises in warm-up and cool-down programmes for horses and riders.

- Specific exercises that are suitable and safe to use to warm up or cool down the main muscle groups.

- The importance of directly relating warm-up exercises to the activity to be performed, e.g. jumping.

3. Why learning styles are important

Everyone is an individual and as such learns information and skills in a different way.

In order to get the best from pupils and assist them in learning new skills, it is beneficial to understand the basic concepts of learning styles and how to incorporate these factors into training sessions.

If you match your teaching style with the students' preferred learning style you will help your students learn better and more quickly. This will assist them to perceive and process information, improving the way they organise and present information.

This is considerably more difficult when teaching group lessons because it is unlikely that all your students have the same preferred style of learning. Therefore it is recommended that you use a combination of teaching methods to ensure you cater for all your students' needs. Although most people have a stronger preference for one style of learning they often learn new skills using a mix of learning methods. To accommodate students' different learning styles it is important that you present new information in a variety of ways.

In practical lessons this is likely to include verbal instructions and short demonstrations followed by an opportunity to try the activity for themselves. Giving students an opportunity to reflect on their performance and ask questions is a very important part of feedback. This information can be used to further improve the effectiveness of future lessons.

There are a number of different learning models: the VAK model is very applicable to horse riders. It is simple to use and most learners can quickly identify their favourite method of learning. It splits learners into three main categories – **visual** learners (V), who like to learn through observing and watching others; **auditory** learners (A), who benefit from verbal instructions and talking about what they have done; and **kinaesthetic** learners (K), who enjoy finding out through actually doing the activity for themselves. A combination of all three methods will assist riders to improve their performance.

Honey and Mumford (1982) have put forward the theory that there are four different styles of learning.

The activist likes to be involved with new experiences. They are open minded and enthusiastic about new ideas but get bored with implementation. They end up doing things and tend to act first and consider the implications afterwards. They like working with others, but tend to hog the limelight.

The theorist adapts and integrates observations into complex and logically sound theories. They think problems through in a step by step way. They tend to be perfectionists who like to fit things into a rational scheme. They tend to be detached and analytical in their decision making.

The reflector likes to stand back and look at a situation from different perspectives. They like to collect data and think about it carefully before coming to any conclusions. they enjoy observing others and will listen to their views before offering their own.

The pragmatist is keen to try things out. They want concepts that can be applied to their job. They tend to be impatient with lengthy discussions and are practical and down to earth.

Many people will show a combination of different learning styles when they learn and not have a clear preference for one particular style. If this is the case then they tend to be able to take in information in a variety of ways and not have many issues. If a person has a strong preference for one particular style then it is useful to know this and you can adapt your coaching to suit this. More and more people nowadays are aware of their preferred learning style so it may be useful to ask them if they know.

With riding a reflector can be a difficult person to teach, because they will always want to stop, analyse and reflect what is happening and sometimes they just need to go and do it and practice. A theorist can be helped by sending them away to read useful books to back up their practical skills. An activist may just want to get on and have a go. They may want to 'run before they can walk' and safety may become an issue.

It is suggested that the following subject areas are suitable to be included in the classroom teaching lecture:-

- Visual, Auditory and Kinesthetic (VAK) learning styles.

- Activist, Reflector, Theorist and Pragmatist learning styles.

- How to accommodate learning styles in a group lesson.

4. Nutritional advice for novice riders

Horse riding can be a very demanding activity; therefore it is important to eat a nutritious, balanced diet to provide sufficient fuel for your body. The base of the diet should come from carbohydrates, in the form of starches and sugars, to give you energy. Protein, fats and vitamins and minerals are also required. This means eating a variety of foods every day – grains, vegetables, fruits, beans, lean meats, and low- fat dairy products are good examples. Fluids, especially water, are very important.

Before exercise, high carbohydrate foods like bananas, will be broken down quickly and provide glucose to the muscles. The timing of meals depends on the rider's preference for eating before exercise, but eating 1 to 4 hours before exercise helps keep plenty of blood glucose available for working muscles. Eating too close to exercising may cause a 'stitch' and can leave the rider feeling uncomfortable. However, it is important to drink plenty of water before exercise to keep muscles hydrated. Good hydration and a well-balanced diet are also thought to help reduce the likelihood of getting cramp. This can be common in the novice rider, who will be more prone to fatigue and may lack general fitness.

During exercise perspiration and exertion deplete the body of fluids and lead to dehydration. Therefore it is important to drink plenty of water, especially in hot weather. The average person needs to drink 1.2 litres (6 to 8 glasses) of fluid a day to prevent dehydration. Dehydration can be very serious. Some of the first signs of dehydration include a dry throat and headaches. If not dealt with, dehydration could lead to confusion and irritability and lack of concentration.

For the novice rider to gain maximum benefit and enjoyment from riding activities they will benefit from having good general health and fitness; this can be assisted with a well-balanced diet.

The overweight rider may be less balanced and flexible and more prone to fatigue and wear and tear on joints and ligaments. If excessively overweight the number and type of horses available for them to ride will be limited.

The following key points are relevant for inclusion in the classroom teaching discussion:

- The components of a balanced diet.

- The importance of sufficient and regular fluid intake.

- The dangers and signs of dehydration.

- The benefits of eating a balanced diet.

- The problems associated with eating to close to participating in riding.

- The problems that can be experienced by the overweight rider.

5. How to deal with parents and carers

Being a parent is a very challenging role. Parents are responsible for their child's safety and general welfare and may from time to time become anxious about their child taking part in riding activities. Occasionally their apprehension and anxiety may negatively effect a child's riding performance and consequently make the child anxious or scared. Conversely some parents can be overly competitive and push their offspring into activities for which the child is insufficiently prepared or experienced to complete. These situations are unfortunate and will require careful and tactful management from the coach. It is important to remember that the parents' conduct is well meaning and they are trying to do what they feel is best for the child. Occasionally their conduct can have a detrimental effect on the child or the rest of the group and it will be necessary for the coach to discuss inappropriate conduct. It is important that the coach demonstrates professional conduct and is polite at all times.

Good relationships with parents and carers will assist in getting the best performance possible from children. By involving parents with lessons, not necessarily by watching, the coach will aid their understanding of the goals you are trying to achieve and help the parent to be supportive without being overly pushy.

Children generally enjoy parents taking an interest in what they are trying to achieve and by involving them the coach helps them to be part of the learning experience.

Taking these key points into consideration, the following topics are suitable for inclusion within the classroom teaching section:

- How to maintain a professional and respectful relationship with parents and carers.

- How to keep parents involved with lessons.

- How to build a good rapport with parents and carers.

- The role of the parent or carer in increasing a child's self confidence.

- How parents/carers can support their child and help improve their performance.

- The importance of regularly speaking to parents/carers.

- Keeping parents/carers safe if observing riding lessons.

- How to deal with an angry or annoyed parent.

- How to manage a parent or carer who interferes or shouts comments to their child whilst observing lessons.

6. Roles and responsibilities of a coach

A coach should try to create a supportive environment in which riders feel confident and are encouraged to give their best performance. In order to achieve this goal there are many aspects a coach should consider. The following list includes many of the areas that could be incorporated within the roles and responsibilities of a coach and therefore could be included in the classroom teaching discussion:

- Preparation, delivery and evaluation of coaching sessions.

- Assessment of horse and rider.

- Adapting lessons to suit the riders and horses needs.

- How to provide a safe coaching environment.

- Methods to develop performance – physical and mental.

- The importance of self-reflection and evaluation of coaching sessions.

- Health and safety considerations when delivering a practical session.

- Child protection and duty of care.

- Clear and effective methods of communication.

- How to create a learning environment.

- How to advise and safely direct helpers.

- The importance of feedback.

- Safe and ethical coaching practice.

- The importance of planning equipment and resources for practical lessons.

- Advising the beginner rider on safe and appropriate clothing and conduct.

- The importance of conducting a risk assessment.

- Being a role model.

What the assessor is looking for

- You must be able to give your presentation in a clear controlled voice, showing some variation in tone and volume if necessary (Element 5.2.1).

- Your body language must show confidence and authority (avoid hands in pockets, looking down and talking into the floor).

- You should try to plan your subject so that you make a brief introduction, then content which includes clear facts and information, followed by a brief summing up and conclusion (Elements 5.1.1 and 5.2.2).

- You should prepare your presentation before your exam day. If you have had the opportunity to practise with an audience, this will help with your confidence.

- Try to ensure that you involve the audience as much as possible and avoid a pure 'chalk and talk' lecture.

How to become competent

- It is important that you feel comfortable when speaking to a small group of people with whom you are not familiar. You must achieve this by practising giving short prepared talks to your friends or co-students, so that you develop competence.

- Gradually try to get some practice in teaching groups of pony club or riding club members on familiar subjects.

- Practise preparing some of the suggested subjects for the presentation so that you have planned the introduction, the subject content, the summary and conclusion.

- Make sure that you practise the timing. There is not very long and it is important not to hurry to finish when the assessor asks you to bring the session to a close.

- When the assessor asks you to finish, or tells you that you have a minute or two remaining, make sure that you finish the sentence you are starting smoothly and with no change in the pace of your voice. Then state that you have no time left or have been asked to finish your presentation and ask if there are any questions, before thanking your audience and briefly summing up in your conclusion and asking one or two questions to test for learning.

- Your summing up should only be a sentence or two to conclude the talk; it should not end up being a brief run through of everything you have already said!

- You will probably give your presentation to the other members of your candidate group and the assessor(s) will sit at the back of the room or aside from the group you are addressing.

- Be confident enough to make eye contact with your audience; preferably stand to give your presentation as this carries more impact and authority than if you sit down.

- You may feel nervous and think your voice sounds shaky but to your audience this is rarely the case.

- If it helps to jot down a few bullet points on a postcard to act as prompters for you, this is fine, as long as you do not end up 'reading' your notes without lifting your head and looking at your audience.

- Avoid trying to say too much.

- Do give your presentation clearly and with a confident voice with variation in your voice tone.

- Do introduce the subject clearly.

- Do involve the audience.

- If you use a white board, write clearly, straight and with correct spelling. If you cannot do this then don't use a board.

- Practise giving these brief presentations frequently, if necessary to your friends and family, so that it is easy to do even when you are nervous.

Business Knowledge/Yard Organisation

The candidate should be able to:

Show knowledge of basic organisation of a commercial establishment.

ELEMENT

C **6.1.1** Outline procedures for receiving visitors.

C **6.1.2** List relevant information required from new clients.

S **6.1.3** List appropriate information given out to new clients, including assessment procedures.

C **6.1.4** Describe the minimum clothing requirements for new clients.

C **6.1.5** Give examples of horse/rider allocation, including popular/unpopular horses.

S **6.2.1** Describe suitable methods of recording bookings and payments.

S **6.2.2** Give examples of client retention schemes (money, hats, children's courses, etc.).

C **6.3.1** Describe procedures used to ensure new clients are assessed before joining a hack or ride.

S **6.4.1** Explain client numbers for group lessons and hacks.

C **6.5.1** Describe how to look after riding surfaces and care for jump poles, wings, etc.

What the assessor is looking for

- You should be able to discuss the procedure that your yard adopts for meeting and receiving strangers or visitors to the yard (Element 6.1.1). All yards should have a procedure for receiving visitors. It is vital for security, and for visitors and clients to feel valued, that there is a procedure in place. Visitors should be welcomed with a smile and a 'Good morning/afternoon. Can I help you?' by all staff and students. In many yards staff and students are recognisable by either corporate clothing or a name badge. The office should be clearly marked and new visitors escorted there. Individual yards may have other procedures: for instance visitors are not allowed in close proximity to the horses unless accompanied by a member of staff. Be prepared to talk about any other procedures that are in place in yards that you know.

Enquiries by telephone should be answered politely, helpfully and efficiently. Potential customers should feel at ease and valued. There should be a general procedure for answering the phone. 'Good morning. Seaview Riding School. Mary speaking, how can I help you?' is much more user-friendly than a gruff 'Yes?'

Potential clients will want to know :

- what kind of riding school it is

- the qualifications of the staff

- the types of riding/activities available

- the types of horses/ponies available

- the times the school is open

- the costs

- where the school is

- they should also be informed that any new client is always given an assessment lesson before being put into a group or taken for a hack out

■ You must be able to discuss information that would be essential to your riding school from a new client (e.g. height, weight, previous riding experience if any) (Element 6.1.2).

It is vital that you obtain certain basic information about all new riders. Existing rider documentation should be kept updated. You need to know their height, weight, age (if a child), previous riding experience and if they have any medical problems relevant to riding. You also need to know what their riding ambitions are. All this should be recorded on a rider registration form which must be signed by them.

RIDER REGISTRATION FORM

The British Horse Society

Name of Equestrian Establishment

CONFIDENTIAL - Please complete all Sections and Boxes

First Name: Surname:

Address:

Postcode:

Tel: (Home)   Tel: (Mobile)

Email:

Date of Birth: Age: Weight: Height:

Occupation:

Have you (or the person you are signing for) ever suffered a serious injury or discomfort while riding or been advised not to ride?   Yes [ ]   No [ ]

If yes, please describe:

Please detail **ANY** disability or medical conditions that may affect your ability to ride or which your instructor should be aware of in case of emergency.

EMERGENCY CONTACT & DOCTORS DETAILS

Contact Name & Relationship   Tel:

Doctors Name   Tel:

RIDING ABILITY - you MUST tick all boxes that apply

I consider myself (or the person riding for who I am signing on behalf as a minor) to be a:

Never ridden before [ ]   Beginner [ ]   Novice [ ]   Intermediate [ ]   Advanced [ ]

How many times have you/rider ridden in last 12 months: None [ ]   under 12 [ ]   12-40 [ ]   40+ [ ]

What do you believe yours or the person riding' capabilities to be on a horse or pony to be?

Riding at a walk [ ]   Trotting with Stirrups [ ]   Trotting without Stirrups [ ]   Cantering [ ]

Hacking [ ]   Riding over jumps up to 0.5m (18") [ ]   Over jumps 0.75m (30") [ ]   Riding over cross country jumps [ ]

RIDERS UNDER 16 YRS OF AGE: I accept full responsibility for my child and confirm that the above pre-assessed abilities are correct. I accept my child rides at his/her own risk.
RIDERS AGED 16 YRS AND OVER: I confirm that the above pre-assessed abilities are correct and I agree that **I RIDE ENTIRELY AT MY OWN RISK.**
DATA PROTECTION ACT 1998: Statement: I understand that the information I have given will be held in accordance with the Data Protection Act 1998 but may also be made available to Insurers and other concerned parties in the event of any injury or accident.
I understand that I must obey the instructions of the instructor and must comply with the Health & Safety requirements of the establishments. I reserve the right not ride a horse allocated to me or my child and or request a change of instructor.
I confirm that to the best of my knowledge all the above details are correct. A parent or guardian of riders under the age of 16 must sign this form.

I acknowledge **THAT RIDING IS A RISK SPORT AND HOLDS A POTENTIAL DANGER, and that all horses may react unpredictably on occasions.**

If signing on behalf of rider please state relationship to rider:

Signature   **Print Name**   **Date**

TO BE COMPLETED BY INSTRUCTOR / SUPERVISOR ON BEHALF OF THE EQUESTRIAN ESTABLISHMENT

This client has been assessed and our judgement of their capabilities is as follows:

Complete Beginner (Lead rein/Lunge) [ ]   Beginner (Beginning Walk & Trot independently) [ ]

Novice (Walk, Trot, Canter independently) [ ]   Intermediate (Jumping, Stage 1) [ ]   Advanced (Stage 2, Equivalent and above) [ ]

ASSESSMENT LESSON CONTENT: Walk [ ]   Trot [ ]   Canter [ ]   W/O Stirrups [ ]   Jump [ ]   Lateral [ ]

OFFICE USE - Assessment Lesson

Horse Used   Lesson Type

Date   Time

Signature   **Print Name**   **Position**

- If a new client is starting to ride at your school you should be able to discuss with the assessor what information you would give to the client to help them feel at home when they come for their first riding lesson (Element 6.1.3). You should also be able to discuss your assessment procedure for a new client, to enable you to fit the person into the most appropriate lesson situation.

The BHS produces an induction pack that riding schools are encouraged to use with clients. This explains riding from the health and safety aspects and gives new riders the opportunity to understand the risks involved in riding and how they can be minimised.

All new clients should be assessed before they are allowed to join a class or go out on a hack. Some riding schools make the assessment the first lesson; others have a short assessment period before the lesson proper or the hack out. New clients should be informed when they book in that they will be assessed. Invariably, riders who are happy to do this will be at the level they say they are, and those who are not so happy are the ones who think they can ride but do not possess the appropriate level of skill.

There is a wealth of information that you could give to new riders, so you must be sure that they are not overloaded and therefore unable to remember everything. There is a first-class leaflet from the BHS entitled: *'Are you starting to ride?'* which may be useful to have on hand to give to new riders.

It is vital to stress that jewellery should not be worn while riding. An easy way to convince people that they should not wear their largest gold-hooped earrings is to point out that not only are they a potential danger, but that they may also get lost in the school floor, never to be found again.

New riders cannot be expected to go out and purchase a set of riding gear – after all, they may have two or three lessons and then decide that riding is not for them.

Many riding schools hire out hats for new clients to wear and encourage riders to purchase their own hat as soon as they are sure they wish to continue with riding. Hats must be to current BSI standards and well maintained. If a school hat is dropped on the floor then it must be replaced, just as you would replace your own.

Riders should be encouraged to wear comfortable trousers – jeans are not really suitable as the seam on the inside of the leg is thick and can rub a rider's inner thighs. Jogging bottoms or leggings can be good if they are thick enough. Tight trousers are not suitable for obvious reasons. Clients must not be allowed to ride in shorts no matter how hot the weather.

Loose-fitting clothing that does not flap about is good for upper wear. Long sleeves are advisable, as they protect the skin of the arms in the event of a fall.

If riding outside, a waterproof coat is essential in wet weather.

Footwear is very important. Some riding schools hire out riding boots as well as hats. Stout lace-up shoes (for a child - school shoes) are acceptable. They must have a small, solid heel to stop the foot slipping through the stirrup. Buckles can catch on the stirrup; and fashion shoes are not strong enough. Trainers should not be allowed as there is no heel and they are not substantial enough. Wellingtons and boots with a thick-ridged sole are not good as the rider's foot can get stuck in the stirrup. Invariably with a beginner rider there has to be some give and take, but safety should never be compromised.

All riders should be encouraged to wear gloves as this will protect their hands from the reins and from the cold in inclement weather conditions.

If not jumping, body protectors should be optional. Again, some riding schools hire them out; others insist that if riders wish to wear them they must purchase their own. It is advisable for riders who are going to jump to be encouraged to wear them. If going cross-country they should be mandatory as they are in competitions.

- You may be asked to discuss how you allocate horses to your pupils; this would include information about how you encourage riders to ride a range of horses in your school, including those they love and those that they are not so keen to ride (Element 6.1.5).The allocation of horses and ponies to pupils is done in different ways, usually depending on the size of the establishment. It is vital that horses and ponies are not overworked and that their work load is varied so they do not become sour. A horse that is particularly good as a beginner's mount or is a really good lunge horse must be given the opportunity to hack out and be ridden by more experienced riders.

The number of hours a horse works per day depends on the type of work he is doing. A horse working at Stage 4 level may only be able to do two hours per day, but a horse undertaking less strenuous work may be able to do four hours a day as long as the work is spread throughout the day. All horses should have a day off a week. Some schools close for one day, others rotate horses' days off.

Beginners are best riding the same horse until they feel safe and confident. Riders tend to have their favourite mounts and sometimes it is difficult to convince them to change. If a hobby rider does not want to change then, although it would be better for their long-term progression to ride different horses, they should not be coerced into riding different horses. Riders who wish to progress, take exams or just continue to improve must ride a variety of horses to enhance their feel and technique. Often within a riding school there is one horse or pony that is not particularly popular, for whatever reason. Riders can be encouraged to ride this animal by employing a little psychology. By telling clients that you want them to ride this animal because they are going to help to improve it, or because you feel it will really help some particular part of their riding, or by using some other positive comments, you can often win them over.

If it is a real problem to convince clients to ride a particular horse or pony, then perhaps the school should consider selling him. It must be remembered that a client is a customer, and if customers do not like the experience they receive they are unlikely to return. (For example: there must be a shop or restaurant you will not go into because of the quality of service you have received).

When allocating horses it is important for the horses' sake that the tasks they undertake vary. Just because a horse is a good lunge horse does not mean he should do lunge lessons every day. He will soon become a poor lunge horse. Organising small shows on site, gymkhana games and obstacle courses can really help to help keep both clients and horses keen and interested. Many centres will not allow clients to take horses off site for competitions because of the risk of injury and/or the loss of revenue.

- You will have questions on methods of booking clients and taking payment for lessons (Element 6.2.1). Each school will have its own method of recording bookings and payments. A booking-in sheet should be as simple as possible so there is no possibility of mistakes being made. Some schools use a book similar to those used in hairdressers', with the instructors' names at the top of each column. Others use a simple diary. At some schools only certain members of staff are allowed to book in clients; at others any member of staff who is trained may book in clients. It is important that no mistakes are made. A client who arrives for a lesson at a given time will not be very happy if they find there have been changes made. There should be a cancellation policy for both the school and clients. Both parties should strictly adhere to this. Many riding schools have a policy of insisting that any lesson not cancelled 24 hours in advance must be paid for.

You will have questions on methods of booking clients and taking payment for lessons (Element 6.2.1). Payment is usually made before the lesson. Monies received should be recorded. Some schools have a till with a receipts payment roll, which also means that the client receives a receipt. Other schools simply write the payment in a column in the booking-in register and this is added up at the end of each day and checked against the monies taken. Money should be securely stored and banked regularly.

- You may be asked about client retention schemes and you should have ideas on these (Element 6.2.2). You should be able to talk about 'pony for the day' days, incentive schemes to encourage riders to book several lessons in advance or reduction schemes on courses or lessons booked in 'bulk'.

There are many ways in which riding schools can try to retain their clients. Probably the best way is to ensure that staff are friendly, interested in the clients, the school is well organised, and the horses are of a good standard and are right for the jobs they have to undertake. Other ideas such as working towards qualifications whether they are the BHS Stages, Progressive Riding Tests, Riding and Road Safety Test or the Horse Owners' Certificates can keep clients engaged. Holding small internal competitions can provide a real focus for those who have a competitive streak. An 'own a pony/horse' day or week can be demanding to organise and run and requires adequate staff and facilities for success, but such days are usually well attended and can be lucrative. Hacks out can keep riders and horses positive. Some riding schools have incentive schemes for clients to purchase lessons in advance in bulk – for example, they may purchase six lessons and get one free. This has the advantage of money being available in advance and there is less administration to do at the beginning of each lesson.

- You should be able to discuss procedures for assessing clients prior to taking them for a hack (Element 6.3.1).

  If any riders are assessed as not competent enough to hack out, they should be offered a lesson instead. On arrival, they should fill out the usual rider registration form and, if wishing to hack out, they should be assessed in the paces they will be riding on the hack. It is also important to assess their confidence, as this can affect the decision as to whether or not it is safe to take them out.

- Have some ideas about how many riders should be taken in one riding lesson (Element 6.4.1). This may vary according to the level of competence of the riders, the ability of the instructor, the nature of the work they hope to do (e.g. an advanced lesson taken by an experienced instructor might have six to eight riders, whereas a less experienced instructor may only be able to cope with three or four riders).

- It is important that the riding surface be kept in good condition. If a track appears around the outside of the school this should be filled in daily to ensure the horses' fetlocks are not constantly being twisted. Different surfaces need different maintenance. All surfaces must be kept flat. If they need watering to stop dust this must be undertaken as often as is necessary. This may be twice a day in hot weather. Dusty surfaces are bad for horses', riders' and coaches' lungs. Some surfaces need harrowing regularly to prevent them becoming 'dead' to ride on. Others need the droppings picked up to maintain the quality of the surface.

- Kickboards should be kept clean, as should mirrors and the gallery (if one exists). If there are notice boards these should be kept up to date and tidy. Nothing looks worse than a notice board with dog-eared pieces of dirty paper pinned to it in a haphazard manner.

- Equipment used regularly on a surface must be kept tidy and safe. Jump wings and poles can be expensive and if they are well maintained they will last longer. They should be regularly painted. Poles can be stored on the walls of an indoor school or on a rack outside an outdoor surface. Wings should only stay in the school if they are going to be used that day. 'Bloks' are really versatile as they can be used for jumps and obstacle courses. Anything made of plastic will eventually crack if left out in the elements for too long. Equipment that is well maintained and stored tidily helps to give the impression of a well-run establishment where people care.

How to become competent

- It is essential that you gain some experience in a commercial riding school, even if you are only able to assist at the weekend, it is still the most valuable way of seeing the clientele of a centre and dealing with the day-to-day issues.

- Find out where the school sources its new clients. Does it regularly advertise in the local press or do riders come through recommendation and word of mouth?

- Are new clients encouraged to come and visit the centre and speak face-to-face with a member of staff? They should be shown around the yard so that they feel familiar with where they will come for their first lesson. They should be shown where the office is, where the loo or rest room is, where the indoor or outdoor arena is and where the horses are.

- There should be a system in place which enables clients to see which horse they have been allocated. In their early lessons, a client should have a member of staff available to help find the horse and bring it out to the school and mount. Many schools have a daily sheet which is displayed on a prominent noticeboard for all to see. Ask if you can become involved in the preparation of this daily sheet so you are able to learn what is required. New clients should have a member of staff available to help them understand the sheet and to get their horse for them and help them mount until they are confident with the processes and regulation involved.

- Be aware that a new rider should be advised on what is safe and appropriate clothing for riding. Do not assume that they will know that a correctly fitting riding hat of a current BSI safety standard is essential. Make sure that you know whether your school hires hats to the client or not, or whether they may borrow one for the first few lessons before being advised to invest in their own.

- Be able to advise on safe footwear, either riding boots, paddock boots or sturdy walking type shoes with a small heel, preferably laced and without a heavy ridged sole. Wellington boots and trainers are not safe, as they may get stuck in a stirrup or slip through respectively.

- Learn to accumulate information systematically from any or all of your clients to include, name, address, contact telephone numbers, age, a person to contact (especially with children) in an emergency. Approximate height, weight, previous experience if any. Any disabilities or medical issues, e.g. asthma, diabetes.

- Information that the client should receive from you (the centre) would include advice on clothing as listed, procedure on arrival at the school (e.g. book in the office and pay in advance).

- Your aim should be to make your clients feel supported and comfortable about coming to the school, but nevertheless clear about the rules in the centre (e.g. no feeding tit-bits to any horses, only bring horses to the school when instructed to do so by your instructor).

- Get to know the booking process of your centre. If you can, become involved in this so you can see how double booking is avoided and non-peak times are filled. Check the cancellation policy of your centre. Some centres do not enforce this policy strictly – if so, find out why this is the case.

- Find out what the payment policy is at your centre and why that policy has been adopted. Whatever it is, it must be clear, understandable and accountable.

- Discuss with your centre any incentive schemes they have for clients. Try to become involved in assessments that are taking place as well as assisting with lessons and hacks. The more practical hands-on experience you get the more practical your answers will be. You will then show the assessor that you are experienced and understand what is involved.

- Discuss with your instructor what his/her feelings are about class numbers. If you are at a riding school then discuss with the proprietor or chief instructor the reasons for the lesson sizes they adopt. The decision has to be a balancing act between commercial viability, health and safety issues and the experience of coach and riders.

- Volunteer to act as a second escort on hacks. This will help you to understand the potential problems and how they can be prevented. It will also help you to understand the matter of horse allocation and customer service. There is a fine line between keeping some customers satisfied and ensuring that health and safety issues are kept as a priority.

Teaching Theory

The candidate should be able to:

Show a sound knowledge of basic equitation and be able to give clear explanations of lesson subjects and teaching format for the standard required for Stage 2 Riding.

Evaluate the worth of different types of lessons.

Show an understanding of organising and escorting hacks.

Show understanding of how rider fitness will impact on the lesson progress.

Show understanding of lesson structure and content.

Show ability to assess rider progress.

Show knowledge of accident and emergency procedures.

The teaching theory section covers a wide range of topics. For ease of reference in this publication it has been split into teaching riding and jumping, sports psychology and safety. Generally all these areas will be covered in the same section on the day of the exam.

ELEMENT

S	**7.1.1**	Outline the advantages and disadvantages of pupil grading systems.
C	**7.2.1**	Describe how to brief assistants when giving a group lesson to lead-rein riders.
S	**7.3.1**	Explain the advantages/disadvantages of private, class, lunge, lead-rein, horse-care lessons and hacks for pupils.
C	**7.4.1**	Describe an escort's responsibility for the ride with regard to control and safety on highways, open spaces and bridleways.

C **7.5.1** Give examples of factors which may lead to discomfort or distress in the horse or rider.

C **7.5.2** Give a description of a child rider experiencing too much physical effort and/or give the possible effects of demanding too much of adult riders.

C **7.6.1** Outline the general format of a lesson.

S **7.6.2** Describe a logical progression of lessons from beginner to Stage 2 Riding on the flat and/or jumping.

C **7.7.1** Give examples of when riders should hold: the saddle, neck strap, reins.

S **7.8.1** Give examples of activities designed to make learning fun for children.

S **7.9.1** Describe how to teach new exercises.

C **7.10.1** Describe and give examples of how to explain and teach the jumping position to riders.

C **7.11.1** Explain the benefits of: ground poles, placing poles, grids, related distances.

C **7.11.2** Give suitable distances for ground poles, placing poles, grids and related distances.

C **7.12.1** Discuss and/or give examples of how to motivate riders.

C **7.12.2** Give rules of use for indoor/outdoor arenas, schooling paddocks, jumps and cross-country fences.

C **7.13.1** Discuss a safe procedure to be followed in case of an accident.

C **7.13.2** Outline the necessity for keeping records of accidents/incidents.

What the assessor is looking for (teaching riding and jumping theory)

This section is assessed with the candidates in a group of up to five. The session takes the form of a discussion between the assessor and the candidates and it is important that you try to contribute on as many different subjects as possible.

- You may be asked about grading riders at different levels of ability (Element 7.1.1). Consider the advantages (e.g. everyone working at the same standard, work chosen by the teacher can suit everyone) and also consider some of the disadvantages (e.g. no one of a higher standard within the ride to demonstrate a new exercise or piece of work for the other riders). Sometimes, in spite of all being the same standard some riders may be more ambitious and hard-working than others.

It is very useful to grade clients into riders that are of similar ability. It is easier for the coach to help the group as they can all work on similar issues. The horses will also all tend to be of a similar standard and this will mean that no horse or rider will be overfaced.

If you have a ride of mixed ability riders, the better riders may become bored and the less experienced riders may feel, at best, incompetent, and, at worst, overfaced, worried and demoralised. It is important that the exercises the ride is asked to undertake are geared at the level of the rider of the lowest ability. Consequently you can see how easy it would be for a very experienced rider to become dissatisfied with their lesson. It is useful, however, sometimes to have a more experienced rider in a lesson if you wish to have particular exercises demonstrated. A better rider can also act as a role model for other riders to aspire to.

Riders of a similar standard can encourage each other in their lessons and out of lesson time. They can share their issues and then realise that they are not the only ones who find certain activities difficult.

Some riders will progress more quickly than others, and as riders improve their goals may change. In these circumstances riders may wish to change groups and this should be discussed with those responsible for group organisation.

It is important to assess new riders before putting them into a group. Many riders overestimate their own capabilities. New riders coming into an established group can help to refresh the ride, but if they are not of a suitable standard then this can lead to the existing riders becoming disgruntled. It must always be remembered that as riding instructors, teachers/coaches we are offering a service to the public and as such they must be treated as valued customers. If they become unhappy they will leave and take their custom to another riding school.

- You may be asked about leaders for beginner riders in a class lead-rein lesson (Element 7.2.1). You should be able to talk about the age and competence of these helpers and that they would be the responsibility of whoever was teaching the lesson.

If you have a group of leaders for a beginners' ride it is important that they understand what they should do. They are there to ensure the riders' safety and control the ponies when necessary. They are not there to teach the riders. It is confusing for the riders if two people are telling them what to do. The helpers should be told that they must only pass on an instruction that you, as the coach, ask them to. You may, for example, ask them to help a beginner to hold the reins correctly, but they should only undertake this when you request it.

When they are leading a pony they must ensure that they have control and that they are concentrating on what is happening. It is a very responsible role to be the leader of a beginner rider and leaders should be encouraged, thanked and praised. You may suggest to them that perhaps they would like to work towards their UKCC Level 1 qualification. Candidates can register for this qualification at the age of 14, although they cannot take the final assessment until the age of 16.

- You will be asked in some detail about different types of lesson (Element 7.3.1). Have some ideas about the value of individual lessons as compared with class lessons; there are always disadvantages as well as advantages (e.g. the advantage of one-to-one individual help needs to be weighed against the possible demoralising effects on pupils who have no one to compare themselves with).

There are several different types of lesson that a customer can choose from. A private lesson ensures that a rider has one-to-one attention and tuition from the coach. Private lessons are very good for novice riders until they are at a standard where they can control a horse competently and are confident enough to join a group. Private lessons are also useful for riders who wish to take their riding very seriously and possibly go on to compete. Private lessons can also build up a rider's confidence quickly as the exercises used will be specific to the individual. They are, of course, more expensive, which can be an issue for some riders. They are also more intensive, so may be of a shorter duration – maybe three quarters of an hour rather than an hour.

- Be clear on the value of a – possibly costly – individual lesson (e.g. for a serious competition rider) versus a group lesson, where there can be camaraderie, motivation to be as good as your friend and a fun social experience.

A class lesson is more social for the riders and can be less intense. The riders have an opportunity to build up a relationship with each other, and can learn by watching each other. The coach needs to be very well organised and ensure that everybody is catered for. All the riders need to feel that they have achieved something during the lesson and that it has been worthwhile for them. Healthy competition between riders can help with progress, but riders can, however, become demoralised if they observe others who constantly seem to be better than they are. Class lessons can easily be made fun for riders who ride for leisure. A class lesson is more viable for a centre, but it is important that the maximum number of riders is restricted so that each rider is happy with the attention they receive.

- Understand the value of beginners starting to learn to ride on a lead rein (or perhaps even the first time on a mechanical horse) or on the lunge.

Lunge lessons are very good for helping the rider to improve their position. Because the coach is responsible for the way the horse goes, the rider can concentrate on his or her own body. A complete beginner may not always benefit from a lunge lesson – if they are nervous or worried they may find it difficult to relax when the person in control of the horse is at the other end of a long rein holding a big whip! A lunge lesson can be intense for both horse and rider, and the coach must ensure that they do not overwork either of them. A novice rider can make huge strides in their position with a few lunge lessons, and the more serious rider can keep their position polished and workmanlike by being lunged. Lunge lessons are usually only half an hour's duration because of the intensity of the work.

For a beginner adult or child lead-rein lessons are a very useful way of starting. An adult may only need one or two lead-rein lessons to get them started, but the confidence gained from having somebody nearby and helping to control the horse can be very important. For adults, a lead-rein lesson may be better as a private lesson as older people can be embarrassed about their lack of ability to undertake new tasks. Many riding schools have class lead-rein lessons for beginner children. As long as there are enough leaders then this is a viable and fun way of introducing children to riding. Without the leaders it is very difficult to have the control necessary, and a beginner class lesson with children who are not being led, can be chaotic.

- Be able to discuss the value of class lessons, individual lessons, group hacks and practical or theory stable management or horse-care sessions.

Class and private lessons are discussed above. It is useful to have stable management sessions available for customers to learn how to look after horses and ponies correctly. Many riders will eventually want to own their own horse and will appreciate having the opportunity to learn the skills required. Riders can be encouraged to take the Progressive Riding Tests and the Horse Owners' Certificates. This can also be a useful income stream on days when the weather is too bad to ride or there are other circumstances where horses are unavailable. If customers learn the skills correctly it will also be beneficial for the welfare of the horses at the school as they will be more correct and consistent in their handling.

Hacking out is something that many riders aspire to and can also be beneficial for the horses. The majority of riders have no desire to become top competition riders and use their riding as a form of stress buster. What better way to relax than to take a hack out in the fresh air on a well-behaved horse.

- Be clear about your responsibility if you were escorting a hack on the roads, open spaces or bridleways (Element 7.4.1). It is important, through the initial assessment and subsequent booking of a hack, that the pupils know exactly how competent they should be (e.g. able to walk, trot and canter independently) before hacking, and that they must take some responsibility for their own control and safety on the ride.

The organisation of a hack must be carefully considered and horses and riders must be carefully matched. The person in charge of the hack must be very experienced and it is advisable for them to hold at least the BET Assistant Rider Leader qualification. If riders were hacking often on the road then the Riding and Road Safety Test would be an advisable option to train for and achieve.

If the riders are not known to the riding school they must be assessed before being allowed out in all the paces that will be used on the hack. The usual rider registration forms must have been filled out. With a group hack it is always best to have a rear escort as well as a leader, who should be the person with overall responsibility. The leader is responsible for the safety of the riders and horses and the paces and the terrain covered must be suitable for the person of the lowest ability to cope with.

Before leaving for the hack, riders' attire and stirrup lengths must be checked, along with the rest of the horses' tack and tightness of their girths. The riders should be informed of the rules they have to abide by. The most important rule is that they must do as they are told by the leader. The second most important rule is that they must not overtake the rider in front of them. To ensure this is successful the horses must be placed in order with the most forward-thinking ones at the front. The leader must tell those who are left at the school where they are going and how long they will be out. They should take a pack out with them that includes a mobile phone or money for a phone box and a simple first-aid kit and a hoof pick. It is also useful to take a lead rein in case it becomes necessary to lead one of the horses. The leader and rear escort must know the riders' names so they can communicate with them quickly to give advice and/or commands.

The leader must set the pace and always let the ride know when they are going to undertake a transition and ensure these are done safely. If a leader suddenly stops it can cause the rest of the ride to 'crash' into them and create a 'domino effect'. If the ride is going to canter then the location must be carefully selected. The best place is a slight uphill path that is fairly enclosed on both sides so that overtaking is not possible. Such an ideal place may not be available, but it may be possible to canter parallel to a hedge, which would help with control. It is better not to canter on the way home.

Hacking out can be difficult when there are only a limited number of rides and canter places. Horses, being creatures of habit, can start to anticipate a canter, become excited and start to misbehave. Riders usually like to have a canter and feel cheated if they don't. It may be useful to take staff out on the hacks and not to canter in the usual places to help break the routine of always doing the same thing in the same place.

The leader and back-up rider should stay alert at all times, observing the riders and looking out for hazards.

It is important when riding on the roads to have knowledge of the Highway Code and to follow its rules. When riding in the countryside always follow the Country Code. The most important points are: always leave gates as you found them; keep to designated paths; ride round the boundary of a field and do not disturb livestock; walk when riding near pedestrians; and do not overtake other riders without their permission.

- You may be asked about factors in a lesson that might contribute to the horse or rider feeling uncomfortable or anxious (Element 7.5.1). Consider the intensity of the lesson with riders who may only ride once a week. Physically they may not be very fit if they do not take any other exercise at all. Even walking the dog, walking to the bus or a weekly swim helps the rider's overall fitness. Hot weather may cause the horses to sweat excessively and therefore become distressed if work is over demanding. The horse may already have done two hours' work during the day and the lesson content should take into consideration the horse and rider's ability to fulfil the work chosen.

- The assessor will expect you to recognise when a child or adult rider is not coping physically or mentally with the work of the lesson (Element 7.5.2).

It is important that, as a coach, you are aware of how your riders are feeling. If they become distressed or are in discomfort they may not tell you. They just will not turn up for their next lesson. Many riders will not tell you if they are in pain or are finding exercises really difficult. Always remember that many riders will not be as fit as you are. A rider's physical shape must be taken into account and this needs to be considered when allocating their mount. For instance, a person who has a short leg length may find a wide cob uncomfortable to ride.

It is easy to ask too much from a beginner or novice rider. Asking for sitting trot for too long, working for extended periods without stirrups, or pushing too hard when trying to teach the rising trot can all lead to a rider becoming physically exhausted. Once the body becomes tired a rider will not be able to control what they are doing so well and progress will be slow. Signs that a rider is becoming physically and/or mentally tired include not being able to maintain the body in the required position, red or very pale face, lack of concentration, shortness of breath, not being able to remain still, facial expression, crying and shortness of temper.

Riders who are worried about something may well talk a lot or may be quieter than usual. They may also stress the fact that they can't do this or that, focussing on their inadequacies rather than their abilities. A rider who is nervous may flatly refuse to ride a particular horse or ask not to try exercises that are out of their comfort zone. Such a request must be respected. If a rider is not happy to try an exercise then the chances they will not be successful are high.

Very hot and very cold weather can create issues. If the weather is very hot the rider may start to become dehydrated and lose concentration and body strength. Very cold weather can lead to the rider becoming stiff and losing feeling in their fingers and toes. Nobody can concentrate in these circumstances! It is vital that you stay alert to signs of distress. In a private lesson a rider may discuss this with you, but in a class lesson they may be too embarrassed to talk about this. Some children will go away from a lesson in real pain and not tell you, whereas others will let you know as soon as there is a trivial issue. It all comes down to observing and getting to know your clients. Building up a good relationship and rapport is essential. Always treat your riders as you would like to be treated yourself.

Weekly riders may well arrive for their lesson thinking about issues that have nothing to do with riding. An adult may have had a particularly difficult day at work, or a child might have had a mishap in the playground that day. These issues can mean that they will be unable to concentrate fully on their riding and are tense and unsettled. This may lead to exercises not being carried out correctly, which in turn may lead to frustration and further tension.

Some mature beginners may not be able to achieve the 'classical' position. As coaches it is important for us to realise that stiffness may be a real issue and that the 'ear–shoulder–hip–heel' line may be totally unachievable. As a coach you must be prepared to compromise and try to ensure that the rider works towards achieving the best position they can, working towards achieving harmony with the horse they are riding. There is a world of difference between teaching a leisure rider and somebody who wants to become a professional in the equine industry and/or a competitor.

■ You should be able to describe the general format of any lesson (Element 7.6.1). Be clear that any lesson of any duration must have an introduction and a period of warming up both horse and rider; during this time an assessment can be made of both the rider's ability and how appropriate the horse is for the rider. The main content of the lesson will be chosen on the findings of the assessment and the latter part of the lesson should include a clear summary of the work and a conclusion so that the rider(s) go away with confidence and understanding of what to aim for or be able to work for the next time.

The general format of a lesson (Element 7.6.1) is the same for whatever the length of session. All lessons should be pre-planned and have a structure so that there is a logical sequence and the riders feel they are progressing.

There are four main phases of a lesson:

The Introduction During the introduction the coach should introduce himself or herself and, if they do not know the riders and the horses, should find out some information about each rider and horse. There should be a brief tack check, including the girths and equality of stirrup length, and the riders' clothing should be observed. The aims of the lesson should be discussed and, depending on the level of the lesson, there could be some discussion with the riders as to which exercises they could use. There could also be a discussion as to whether or not the riders have undertaken any loosening exercises before mounting.

The ride should then be warmed up. This is an important time for horse, rider and coach. This period should consist of simple exercises to supple muscles and tendons in both the horses and riders, and the coach can also use it as a time of assessment. Girths can be re checked and stirrups altered if necessary.

The main lesson content During this phase the main aim of the lesson is worked towards and hopefully achieved. Whatever the lesson content, it must always be relevant to the levels and capabilities of the riders and coach. The work should progress logically and the ride must be given short rest periods so they do not become fatigued. Rest periods must be used tactfully as riders may feel they have spent a lot of time standing still and doing nothing. If a new topic is to be taught then do remember the different ways in which people learn (see pages 50 to 52). Any new topic should be explained and demonstrated and then the riders should be given ample opportunity to practise, practise, practise. It is only by repetition that a new skill can be learnt and assimilated.

As a coach you may well need to have several different ways of putting the same point over, and have patience to help riders improve. To ask a pupil to repeat the same thing in the same way, over and over again, can become de-motivating for that rider. Take every opportunity to observe high-quality coaches and assimilate good ideas into your own repertoire of teaching skills.

The conclusion During this phase the riders and horses should be given the opportunity to 'cool down' by undertaking some stretching work. There should be discussion of what has been learned, and the coach should check the riders' knowledge and understanding by asking questions. The riders should be given an opportunity to ask questions. Each rider should be given feedback as to how they have done and a brief action plan as to how they can move forward during the next session. If the coach has assessed the situation as safe, all this could be done at walk on a long rein, which would aid the cool-down process.

Self-reflection The final part of the lesson is where the coach takes the opportunity to self-reflect on how the session has gone. This is absolutely vital if we are to improve our techniques and become better coaches. Always look for the positives first and remember to take these forward for a similar lesson in the future. Then look for the things that did not go as well as you thought and try and work out why this was. Was it because the exercise was too hard for the riders/horses? Were the riders distracted by something? Were the horse and rider combinations unsuitable? Were you explanations muddled? The list is endless. Only by deciding where things went wrong (if they did) can we work to ensure the same issues do not happen again.

- You may be asked to describe a logical progression of lessons from beginner to Stage 2 riding on the flat and/or jumping. (Element 7.6.2).

When making a long term plan for a rider it is important to ensure that you do not assume any prior knowledge. When a beginner comes for their first lesson they may well not know what a girth or the pommel are. There is a huge equine language which those in the industry use daily, but which newcomers have to learn. If we are not careful, a beginner can quickly start to feel inadequate before they have even mounted the horse.

There is no one sequence in which riders should be taught, but there are basic principles that must apply. The most important factor to be taken into consideration is the safety of the rider and horse.

A beginner may well start with lead-rein lessons. They will initially be taught how to check their stirrup length and girth and then how to mount. It is easier for a beginner to learn to mount from a mounting block. This is also better for the horse's back and for the saddle. There is a real skill in giving and receiving a leg-up and a beginner will not have the ability to take a leg-up well. Mounting from the ground can be difficult for a beginner as they may not have the 'spring' required to do this. The coach must always check the girth and tack and assist the rider in any way necessary. Some riding schools give beginners the reins straight away, while others make the rider hold the saddle or neck strap until they are a little more confident.

Once the rider is confident in walk they can be taught a little sitting trot. Some riders find it interesting to be taught the sequence of legs as they learn to undertake walk and trot, but others find this is information overload. Once they can feel the rhythm of the sitting trot, the rising trot can be taught. It is easier for horse and rider if they practise the rising technique at the halt and then at the walk before trying it in the trot. The rider should be encouraged to move the hips forward a little as they rise, and not allow the feet to push the stirrups forward. When the rising trot is established and the rider can rise independently of the hands, diagonals can be taught. Some people teach canter before diagonals and others teach trotting poles before canter. As long as there is a methodology that works for you and your horses, that is acceptable.

When teaching diagonals it is easier for a rider to see how the horse's legs move if the diagonal pairs of legs are fitted with different coloured boots or bandages. Although we should work towards the rider feeling the diagonal, it is usually easier initially to teach them to watch the outside shoulder until they have mastered the technique. Once this is established they can move on to starting to feel the movement.

Right from the beginning it is important to involve the rider in their learning and to ask them for feedback on how they are coping and what they can feel from the movement of the horse.

As soon as a rider is confident riding with their stirrups they should be introduced to work without stirrups. This can be in walk initially and built up to trot as confidence increases. Riding without stirrups is so beneficial for balance and position it is something that every rider should be encouraged to try.

Teaching a person to canter is one of the most difficult things to do in riding.

Riding schools will have their own methods for doing this, but it is important that nobody is forced into trying to canter if they do not want to, and that the horses used are the right ones for the job and are schooled for the task. As a coach you cannot expect a rider to remember the complicated aids for canter when they are excited and/or apprehensive about what is going to happen. A rider will need to be told how to apply a basic aid to canter (hold the neck strap/pommel with one hand, sit up and use the legs) and the coach may well have to use their voice to help the horse into the pace. The coach can explain to the rider that as they become more proficient more subtle aids to ask a horse to canter can be applied. A few strides of canter is enough for the first attempt. If the horse canters for too long the rider may well tip forward and lose balance.

School figures: Riders should be encouraged to ride school figures accurately and smoothly, and once they are proficient they should understand how their position and aids can affect the way in which the horse performs these. By learning to ride accurate school figures the rider learns how to prepare a horse for a movement, and self-discipline, which is vital for anyone wishing to become a genuinely educated rider.

Circles are usually of 20m, 15m or 10m diameter. In a 20 x 40 metre arena these are the most usual places to ride them

As riders become more efficient they can be introduced to more difficult figures.

Half circles (see page 25) of various sizes can be used to change the rein.

A 5m loop (see page 25) appears easy, but to ride one accurately and keep the horse in balance while doing so, is a real skill.

A three-loop serpentine (shown on page 25) needs thought and preparation to ensure the horse maintains balance and that the figure is symmetrical.

Once the rider is proficient in canter they may well want to start to hack out. If they have done some work over poles and in the light seat then they can apply this technique while out hacking if the necessity arises.

When introducing jumping it is very important again that the rider wants to learn to jump and that the horse is the right one for the job. More people stop jumping because they have learnt on unsuitable horses and have 'lost their nerve' than carry on and enjoy the skill. If the rider has not already learned the light seat with shortened stirrups then this must be taught first. The rider must learn to be secure through the lower leg in the light seat before they attempt a jump. They should also be happy in the light seat over trotting poles.

A first jump should be a single cross-pole, and the rider must hold a high neck strap whilst attempting this. This is for the sake of the horse as much as for the rider. Once the rider is happy going over a single fence in trot they can move on to a second fence. This fence should not be at a related distance to the first fence. If the first fence is at B (off the track) then the second fence could be off the track at E. This gives the rider plenty of time to rebalance him/herself before attempting a second fence. A third fence can be put across the diagonal, which starts to introduce the idea of a small course. Once the rider is confident putting a small number of fences together they can then be introduced to grid work.

As confidence improves, the height of the fences can be raised a hole at a time until the rider is happy jumping at Stage 2 height. It must be remembered that to pass Stage 2 jumping, the candidate must be confident enough to get on two unfamiliar horses and jump them round a course. This means that they must practise jumping as many different types of horse as possible. A rider who is only happy to jump the same horse will not be successful in Stage 2 jumping.

- Linked into the progression described above, you may well be asked to give examples of when riders should hold the saddle, neck strap and reins (Element 7.7.1).

It is very important that a beginner and novice rider has a neck strap of some kind to use when necessary. As already mentioned some riding schools do not allow beginners to hold the reins until they are capable in rising trot. Other schools allow beginners to hold the reins from the first lesson, but make the riders hold the neck strap with one or both hands for trot work. Sometimes the reins are tied in a knot, and sometimes the rider puts the reins into one hand and holds the neck strap with the other; at other times the reins are slipped through the fingers and the pommel is held at the same time. This can be a huge handful for a child with small hands, so care must be taken.

Riders should be encouraged to hold the front of the saddle or the neck strap whenever they feel unsafe; by doing so they do not interfere with the horse's mouth. If the rider is already behind the movement with their weight distribution then holding the pommel can encourage the weight to go further back, whereas holding the neck strap can encourage the rider to come a little more forward. When deciding whether or not to hold the neck strap, pommel and/or reins the security of the rider and the welfare of the horse are the two main priorities that need to be considered.

- You may be asked to discuss activities that are aimed at giving children fun in lessons (Element 7.8.1).

There are a huge range of activities that can make learning fun for children. Some examples are:

Gymkhana games – mounted and dismounted

Obstacle courses/handy pony

Inter-group competitions

Fancy dress (especially at Christmas/Easter)

Speed exercises – e.g. fastest round the world

Drill/musical rides

Riding to music

'Follow the leader'

'Simon says'/imitating the coach

Learning names of colours/tack/points of the pony, etc.

Touching the school letters and thinking of a word beginning with that letter

Riding round, through, and over poles set in various patterns

Working towards the Progressive Riding Tests

- You should be able to explain how you would teach new exercises (Element 7.9.1).

When a new task is learnt it is important for coaches to understand how it is learnt so that they can help their pupils at each stage and recognise the issues that are there to do this.

It is generally agreed that there are four stages of learning:

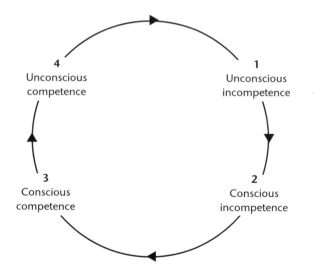

4
Unconscious
competence

1
Unconscious
incompetence

3
Conscious
competence

2
Conscious
incompetence

If we take an example of a person wishing to learn to ride:

Often those who have never ridden think it is easy to do so and they can just 'get on and do it'. This is **unconscious incompetence**. They are unaware of what is involved in the basics of riding and how difficult it is to stay balanced and use the most basic of aids.

On getting onto a horse the first few times they become aware of what is involved and realise that they are unable to make a horse do what they want to do. This is **conscious incompetence**. They realise how many skills are involved and that there is much to learn.

They start to learn skills of using their aids, staying in balance and reacting to the horse they are riding. They have to think carefully about what they are doing and work hard to learn the new skills required. This is **conscious competence**.

As their skills improve they are able to use their new found skills without thinking about them and can start, stop and turn with ease. They have now reached the stage of **unconscious competence**. Once this stage of learning is reached then the rider will be able to move on and learn other new skills through the same process. For instance, once they have mastered the basic aids they may well start to learn to jump or move on to more complicated flatwork.

As a coach you must remember that many of your personal riding skills will probably be at the unconscious competence stage. You must remember that your learners will not be at this stage and will still have many difficulties to overcome. It is a major part of your role to understand this and find ways to help them overcome their issues so that they achieve their goals, enjoy riding and want to continue in their sport.

When teaching new exercises it is important to remember the phases of learning. Different learning styles (see pages 50 to 52) must also be taken into consideration.

You must ensure that riders have the level of competence necessary to learn a new skill. For example, it is no use trying to teach a rider about their diagonals when they are not competent in rising trot. For them to have to concentrate on how to rise **and** work out which pair of legs to rise on at the same time would overload them. This would lead to them being unsuccessful and possibly de-motivated.

Many people will learn something new if they can understand the reason why they need to learn it. So, when explaining a fresh topic, try to put in simple language why there is a necessity to learn the skill. It is very important that any explanation is put into language that is suitable for the riders you are teaching. Children will respond better to simple language that is couched in terms they understand.

After the explanation of the new skill it is important that there is a demonstration of some kind – maybe a member of the group is used, or the coach may demonstrate. It is important to encourage the riders to ask questions to ensure they understand. An open question such as, 'How are you going to attempt this?' is much more useful than a closed question (i.e. one leading to a yes or no answer) such as, 'Do you understand?'

Once the new skill has been explained and demonstrated then there has to be plenty of time for practising. As previously mentioned with such a practical topic there is no substitute for being 'hands on'. The coach may have to find several different ways of presenting the same skill. The riders will then not lose interest and will persevere until the skill is learnt. Throughout the process the riders should be encouraged to discuss what they are feeling and thinking, and be helped to work through any issues they have. When riders are engaged in their learning they will learn more quickly and will better retain the knowledge and skill.

- Elements 7.10.1, 7.11.1 and 7.11.2 deal with the development of jumping, which will be covered in some detail. You must be able to explain the jumping position clearly and how you would teach it. You will be asked about methods to develop the rider's jumping position, and these should include practice of rhythm and pace on the flat and include poles as appropriate. You must understand and be able to explain basic jump distances (e.g. 9ft/2.7m placing pole to a jump if the approach is from trot. A canter approach here is not advisable for inexperienced riders).

To teach a rider to jump, the coach must be confident and competent and the horses/ponies must be used to the task and reliable. The rider must want to learn to jump; do not force anybody to jump who does not want to. They will be negative, stiff and very worried, and this could lead to an accident.

Before a rider starts to jump they must be secure in the light seat. It is possible for riders to become confused when talking about light seat/jumping position. It is important that you describe clearly what you mean to your riders so they understand and are on the same wavelength as you. Light seat generally tends to be described as a position of the upper body between the normal flatwork position and the fold adopted over a jump. It can also be called the poised position, the forward seat or half seat. Some people also call this the jumping

Jumping position. The angle of the upper body can vary according to whether jumping in show-jumping or cross-country pace, as the rider's balance and ability develop.

position and do not distinguish between this 'half-way' position and the fold over a fence. As you can see with all these different definitions and terms it is important that you and the riders understand each other. It is also important that you and the assessor are talking about the same thing.

When teaching the light seat (within this text this term will be used to describe the position that is half way between the fold and the flatwork position), it is important to ensure firstly that the riders shorten their stirrups if they have learned to ride with a long length of leg in their flatwork. It is necessary to close the three joints of hip, knee and ankle, so that the rider's body weight will be able to follow the horse through the phases of the jump (see page 90). If they have learned with a shorter length of stirrup then they may not need to shorten the stirrups until they start to jump above about 18ins/45cm.

Start the rider off by asking them to adopt the light seat in halt. You can demonstrate this from the ground. The upper body inclines forward, allowing the hands and arms to follow the line of the reins, and the hips 'think' slightly backwards. The rider should firstly practise this in halt. It is vital they learn to become secure through the lower leg. The weight must be kept down the back of the leg through supple ankle joints into the heel.

When the rider can maintain this position in halt, they can move into walk. They need to find the place where their upper body is able to maintain balance over their lower leg. This will not be exactly the same upper body position for everybody, and as a coach it is important you understand this. Riders may need to hold the neck strap or mane initially to help them find their balance. Once they can balance in walk they can move on up to trot and then on to canter. They can then progress to work over a single pole and on to a line of poles. The time spent doing this work will be hugely beneficial when the rider starts to actually jump.

A rider should not be allowed to jump until they can balance in the light seat in all three paces and over poles. Too many riders are put off jumping because they are asked to go over fences before they are secure and then become unbalanced, fall off and lose their nerve. Do remember that this will be very strenuous for a rider who is not used to riding in this position. Frequent short rests will be necessary, and the rider may need to take their feet out of the stirrups and stretch their legs.

Once the riders are competent in walk, trot and canter in light seat they can be introduced to pole work. A single pole placed on the three quarter line at E or B is the best pace to start. This means the turn the rider has to make at the end of the school is not too tight and there is plenty of room to make a good straight approach and getaway. If the riders have not done this before it is better to do it individually. As they become proficient they can undertake the exercise as a ride, but must keep three to four horses' distance apart and not come over the pole if it has been knocked out of place by the previous rider. You can then increase the number of poles, which will mean the riders have to stay in balance for longer and will learn to absorb more and more movement from their horses. Pole work also helps to improve a rider's confidence before actually jumping. As jumping is just as much about confidence as it is technique this is vitally important.

There is much discussion about how many poles you should put out after one. It is generally accepted that if the poles are placed 9 ft/2.7 metres apart then you can go from one to two poles. If the poles are placed closer so the horse has to step over a pole every step then it is safer to go from one to three poles. The horse should then not think he has to jump them. The accepted distance for trotting poles for an 'average' horse is 4ft 6ins/1.4m. For a pony it can be as small as 3ft 6ins/1.06m.

You must learn :

(a) how to walk pole and jump distances accurately so you know how large your stride is;

(b) pole and jump distances;

(c) to tell when the distances you have set for horse/ponies is not comfortable for them and be able to alter them so they are safe.

Distances for an 'average' horse of about 15.2hh:

Trotting poles: 4ft 6ins/1.4m

One non-jumping stride between two fences (trot approach): 18ft/5.4m

One non-jumping stride between two fences(canter approach): 21ft/6.4m

One non-jumping stride between two fences (competition distance): 24ft/7.3m

Two non-jumping strides between fences (trot approach): 30ft/9.1m

Two non-jumping strides between fences (canter approach): 33ft/10m

A related distance of three strides with a canter approach: 45ft/13.7m

Bounce fence – no strides between two fences (not to be used with novice riders):
10–12ft/3–3.6m

Placing pole in front of a fence (trot approach) 8–9ft/2.4–2.7m

When placing a pole in front of a fence to be approached in canter, unless you are using the pole to help with a specific problem, it is better to put the pole one or two canter strides away. A placing pole can be very useful for setting up a horse and rider to reach the correct take-off point for the jump.

It must be remembered that the above distances are only a guide to work from and the coach must learn to assess how a horse is working through poles and jumps and alter them accordingly.

Once a rider is confident and competent in the light seat over poles a single fence can be introduced. Again this is best placed on the three quarter line at E or B. A cross-pole is useful as it will encourage the horse and rider to go straight and is not as imposing as an upright or a spread fence.

Once the riders are happy going over a simple cross-pole then this can be changed to an upright. As in any part of teaching riding it is all about practice. It is more difficult with jumping, though, as the actual jump is over quickly and the rider finds it very difficult to think about everything at once, especially if they are worried about the task. It is important to take things as slowly as necessary and not to push the riders on more quickly than they can cope with. Going over the same fence several times may appear boring to you as the coach, but to the rider it will help them to refine their skills and become more confident. It is vital that the horses are able to do this without becoming bored or excited so, as stated earlier, you must have honest, safe and quiet animals. Once the riders are happy over a single fence they can start to think more about the phases of the jump.

There are five phases to the jump:

the approach to the fence

the take-off

the flight

the landing

the getaway (which can be the approach to the next fence)

The rider should understand that a good approach is vital, with rhythm and balance being maintained and with the horse being presented straight at the middle of the fence. The rider cannot, however, be expected to worry about this until they are happy going over a fence. The same applies to the getaway.

The phases of jumping

To progress from one to two jumps it is easier to put a second jump opposite the first one (at E or B) so the rider has plenty of time to organise themselves between fences. They jump the first fence and ride round to the other side of the school to the second fence. When they are competent and confident doing this a third fence can be added across the diagonal. Once a rider is confident doing a 'simple course' like this they can then be introduced to gridwork.

- You will be asked about the benefits of using ground poles, placing poles, grids and related distances. (Element 7.11.1) You must also be able to discuss basic grid construction and how to estimate the distances between one jump and another.

Gridwork is excellent for both horses and riders. It improves the rider's position and can help to increase their concentration. It helps increase suppleness and athleticism in both horses and riders and can help to build up their muscle tone. If the grid is set at comfortable distances for the horse it can help enhance their balance, rhythm, co-ordination and bascule. By changing the distances within a grid a horse can be helped to lengthen or shorten his stride and bascule. This type of gridwork should only be undertaken with very competent and confident riders who can help the horse in his way of going, if necessary, and be able to ride through the grid without detriment to his action.

Gridwork should not be attempted with novice jump riders. Although it may appear easy because the jumps are set so that the horse goes through the grid and the rider just has to follow, if the rider is not secure and well balanced when jumping several jumps, one immediately after the other, they can lose balance and do not have time to regain it. This can lead to a rider fall and/or the horse being yanked in the mouth or the rider landing heavily on the horse's back.

There are many ways a grid can be built. The easiest grid consists of three fences, each at one non-jumping stride apart. Start with one fence, usually a cross-pole to make it inviting and keep the horse central. Asking the riders to approach in trot and land in canter will ensure they have enough impulsion for when the second fence is built. Once the horses and riders are happy going through this, set up the second fence. If there is a trot approach then 18ft/5.4m is a good starting distance for the average horse of about 15.2–16hh. Observe how the horses cope with the distance, and if it is not comfortable then be prepared to alter it. Remember the horses must approach in a forward-going trot that shows impulsion.

When horses and riders are comfortable going through the first two elements then add a third fence. This could be an upright, and the distance may need to be a little longer (approx. 19ft/5.8m) as the horses' frames may well be lengthening a little as they go through the grid. Again, observe whether or not the horses are finding the distance comfortable, and if not (as long as their way of going is forward and rhythmical) then move the fence to make the distance more user-friendly.

If the horses were to approach in canter then the distances between each fence would probably need to be 3ft/90cm longer.

Related distances This is where two fences are placed more than two non-jumping strides apart (which is a two-stride double), up to a distance of about 60ft/18.2m. A three-stride related distance is set at 45ft/13.7m for an easy distance. This can be a straight line or a 'dog leg'. It is no easy task to teach horses and riders to ride related distances well. The quality of the canter – rhythm, balance and length of stride – is vital, as is the line taken by the rider.

Building fences When building a jump always make sure that the fence does not create a false ground line for the horse. When building a fence with a 'dropper' it gives the horse a good guide if you pull the part of the pole that is on the ground forward from the wings a little towards the direction the horse is approaching from.

If there is a pole on the ground acting as a ground line, then again it makes it easier for the horse to take off at a good point if the pole is a few inches forward from the jump itself.

When building spreads for riders who are not very experienced, a cross-pole in front, rather than a straight bar, makes the fence less imposing. Also when jumping a spread that has two straight poles, making the back rail one hole higher than the front rail makes the fence more inviting (known as an ascending spread). A back rail should always be held by collapsible cups.

Never over-face a novice rider. It is always better to make the jump a little lower and put it up one hole at a time as confidence improves.

■ Be sure you understand the rules of use for riding areas. (Element 7.12.2)

To ensure horse and rider safety it is very important that as a coach you pass on the rules for riding when in a group. It is also your responsibility to ensure that all riders in your tutelage abide by them.

These are the accepted rules for when working in an enclosed area:

• If working as a ride keep one horse's distance apart.

• If working in open order pass left to left when meeting somebody who is riding at the same pace as you.

• If riding in open order in walk then stay on an inside track leaving the track free for those going at a faster pace.

• If riding in open order turn across the school to undertake a downwards transition.

• If you wish to enter or leave the arena, then always ask for and obtain permission from those already there.

• If there is anybody within the arena who is having an issue with a horse then stay well way from them at the other end of the area.

• Jump equipment not in use should be stored neatly and safely.

• Jump cups should not be left on wings when there are no poles on them.

• Riding areas must be regularly maintained to ensure the surface is kept as flat as possible.

• Cross-country jumps must be jumped the correct way round. If jumps are flagged, a red flag on the right and a white flag on the left of the jump indicate the correct direction.

• Cross-country jumps and take-off and landing areas must be regularly maintained.

■ You must remember in all your answers to give clear facts, avoid waffling and put across clear ideas that reflect your knowledge and experience.

How to become competent (teaching riding and jumping theory)

- Learn as much as you possibly can by watching other instructors and learning from the way they use exercises to improve horses' and riders' specific problems.

- Discuss with the proprietor of your own riding school or a local school the system they use for grading riders. Some schools will try to grade according to ability, some may use age as a guide so that riders of the same peer group are riding together. Some schools may grade lessons according to the size of horse. In this case ponies would work in one ride, horses in another. This is easier when using jumping exercises (especially grids) when distances for ponies may be too short for horses.

- Be clear on the brief you would give to an assistant who was leading for you while you are giving a group lesson to beginners. Make sure they know how to hold the lead rope so that it is not uncomfortable for the horse, not wrapped round the hand, and short enough to maintain control. Remember to tell them that when they change the rein they should change sides so that they are not trapped between the wall and the horse/pony. They must realise they are responsible for control of the horse/pony and should always maintain at least one horse's distance between themselves and the horse/pony in front. When they are turned in they must make the horses stand still and be far enough from the others to be out of kicking range. Make sure they realise they are there to do as you ask and not to teach the rider.

- Speak to riders about why they have lead-rein or lunge lessons (particularly adults). Find out why riders prefer class lessons or individual lessons. Some riders like the freedom to hack, others far prefer the structure and control of riding in the school.

- Your own experiences as a rider should give you some opinions about the advantages and disadvantages of private, class, lead-rein, lunge, horse-care lessons and hacks.

- If you have the opportunity of escorting some hacks then this can be very good experience. Understand the order in which you might place the riders (e.g. less experienced or nervous closer to you), make sure you have considered the route you are taking and, if necessary, that you have a second escort to assist you. Understand your responsibilities when riding both on the road and on bridleways. Be aware of what you might take with you to ensure support in the case of an emergency (mobile phone, leaving information as to the route you are taking and approximately the time you will be away).

- If your teaching experience covers several months then you should be aware of the variation of seasonal conditions that may cause discomfort or stress in both horse and rider. Cold, wind, wet and heat can all affect the way your rider and/or horse may feel. Overworking horse or rider can also have an adverse affect.

- Be clear on how to discuss lesson plans. Watch other instructors to see how a lesson should develop. All lessons should have a period of warming up, loosening up both horse and rider and preparing them for more serious work. This period also serves to allow you to assess the rider(s) today and give you a foundation for choosing the work for the lesson. The main content of the lesson should then develop and towards the end of a lesson you should avoid starting anything new, which you may not have time to follow through to a pleasing conclusion. The lesson should have a summing up period or conclusion, where work is consolidated and the riders go away with confidence and clear on the work covered. Always spend a little time giving the riders feedback and telling them how they will move forward in their next lesson. Ask the riders for feedback on yourself and work to take on board any constructive criticism they give.

- Make sure that you are clear on all the work that would be included in a rider's ability up to Stage 2 level and similarly consider the standard of Horse Care expected by Stage 2.

- It may not be long since you were working yourself at that level, so it should be easy for you to remember the progression of your own training to this level and feel confident about delivering a similar format to trainees working towards Stage 2.

- Make sure that you have discussed with your own trainer the options as to how and when novice riders should hold the saddle, reins or a neckstrap when learning to ride. Also watch what other instructors do in different circumstances.

- Make sure that you have watched children playing gymkhana games and generally having fun with ponies on 'own a pony day' or at pony club camp.

Children get much amusement in having the opportunity to plait manes and tails, paint hooves and 'dress up' long-suffering ponies in fancy dress.

- Be careful that you can 'walk' a distance accurately, avoid talking about 'my strides'. 'Your' stride should be as near 3ft, or just under 1 metre, as possible so that you can usefully 'walk' distances accurately.

- Be confident about discussing basic distances of trotting poles (4ft 6ins/1.37m), one placing pole to a jump from a trot approach (8–9ft/2.4–2.7m), one non-jumping stride between two small fences from a trot approach (18ft/5.4m).

- The more you have experienced the exercises yourself the easier it is to visualise and help another person to develop the same skill.

- There is no substitute for watching other instructors, learning from what they do and seeing what exercises they use for different situations.

Motivation, goal-setting and coaching styles

Motivation

There are many definitions of motivation, but generally it can be said to be the driver that makes us want to do something. If we are not motivated then we will not want to do something and so will not be successful. For many people riding is a hobby and something to be enjoyed. If it is not enjoyable then there will be no motivation to continue. Many people give up riding because they lose their motivation. As coaches it is important to understand what is motivating our riders. If we can keep motivation high then we will keep them riding. In a commercial situation this is vital to ensure viability as well as to help riders find and keep the same pleasure we get from riding.

There are two forms of motivation:

Extrinsic This form of motivation comes from outside ourselves. It can be from parents, peers, outside agencies and can also include circumstances, situations rewards or punishments.

With children you may well find that there is a great deal of extrinsic motivation.

Parents may well be pushing a child to ride when they do not particularly want to, or they may be trying to push the child to progress too fast. This is a tricky situation that, if identified, may best be dealt with by the most senior member of staff at an establishment. A tactful discussion with the parents may be the best solution.

In a class situation a child could feel peer pressure to try an exercise that they are not happy with. This is one of the reasons that all exercises within a session must be set at a level that suits the least proficient rider. Peer pressure on young people in all walks of life leads to huge issues for children and if we, within riding, can start to make children aware of the fact that they are all individuals in their own right and help to give them self-confidence then we may well be influencing their development in many areas.

Intrinsic Intrinsic motivation comes from the inside. It stems from what we want to do. If we do not have intrinsic motivation to achieve something then it is highly unlikely that it will be successful over the long term.

It is important to try and find out what is motivating your riders. You will then be able to utilise this in your coaching, helping them to improve and stay focused. You also need to find out what they find de-motivating, for example, they might not enjoy riding a particular horse or being pushed out of their comfort zone.

Goal setting

It is important for us to have goals to know where we want to get to and to use as a bench-mark to tell if we have been successful.

A rider can have:

- A 'dream golden goal', e.g. 'I want to win a gold medal at the Olympics of 2012.'

- A long-term goal, e.g. 'I want to compete at Badminton in 2011.'

- A short-term goal, e.g. 'I want to improve the quality of my horse's canter by the end of the month.'

- A session goal, e.g. 'I want to improve the stability of my lower leg over a fence in today's session.'

All goals should be **SMART**:

Specific

Measurable

Achievable

Realistic

Time related

A dream goal may be just that, but it may help to plan out your long-term, short-term and session goals.

Although the example goals above may not be realistic for the weekly rider it is still important for them to set goals. You as the coach should assist in ensuring they are SMART.

All goals should aim to balance challenge and stress to aid development.

Your weekly rider may have a long-term goal of being able to hack out safely by the spring, a short-term goal of learning to jump a single fence by the end of the month, and a single session goal of being able to get the correct canter lead every time they ask for it in the session. These all provide a structure and enable planning and give both you and the rider something to gauge improvements by.

Coaching Styles

How do you coach your clients? Take a few minutes to think about this. Do you always coach in the same way or do you adapt the way in which you conduct a session depending on who you are working with?

Generally there are three agreed coaching styles:

Autocratic

i. Telling: The coach decides on what is to be done. The riders are not involved in the decision making. The coach defines what to do and how to do it.

ii. Selling: The coach decided on what is to be done. The coach explains what is required and the objectives. The riders are encouraged to ask questions to confirm understanding. The coach defines what to do and how to do it.

Democratic:

i. Sharing: The coach outlines the training requirements to the riders. The coach invites ideas/suggestions from the riders. The coach makes the decision based on the riders' suggestions. The coach defines what to do and how to do it.

ii. Allowing: The coach outlines the training requirements to the riders. The coach defines the training conditions. The riders brainstorm to explore possible solutions. The riders make the decision. The riders define what to do and how to do it.

Laissez Faire:

There is little direction from a laissez faire coaching style as this style allows the group to do what they want to and coaches from what is seen.

Coaches will use a variety of styles/types depending on the coaching situation.

In days gone by the majority of riding teaching has been autcratic telling. There is still a place for this method of coaching especially with a group of novice riders whose safety needs to be ensured. They can still, however, be engaged in a session and asked for feedback on what they are feeling and how everything is going. Where a rider is very experienced and working towards something specific there may be a more democratic sharing coaching style. As a coach it is important to be flexible in your approach and be able to use whichever style is appropriate for those you are helping. This is no easy feat when you are just starting in your coaching career, but should certainly be a part of your personal long term action plan.

What the assessor is looking for (motivation, goal setting and coaching styles)

- You may be asked about goal setting and these questions are likely to come in the theory/discussion part of the examination. They may also be touched on when discussing your practical sessions.

- You should be able to explain why a lesson should have an aim or goal.

- Understand that a pupil learning any subject will be able to prepare and plan their development more easily if they have clear aims or goals set out for them.

- Understand that goals may be dream golden, long-term, short-term or sessional (Element 7.12.1).

- Be able to discuss how these goals may be chosen for each rider.

- Consider what a sessional goal might be in a one-hour class lesson of weekly riders (e.g. today we are going to start to learn about diagonals in trot, by the end of the lesson we will aim to have you understanding what diagonals are and how you recognise which one you are riding on).

- Consider and be able to discuss some long-term goals (e.g. by the end of the summer holidays we will aim for you being able to jump a small course of fences).

- Be able to discuss how goals might change. (A long-term goal may be for the rider to enter a competition in six months' time.) A long-term goal may have to change if a rider misses riding due to an unexpected illness or progresses more quickly than anticipated when the goal was set. The goal may then be moved forward or back from the original time scale planned.

- Be able to discuss motivation or enthusiasm to progress (Element 7.12.1).

- Understand and be able to talk about what motivates a rider (seeing other members of the peer group progressing, friends or family inspiring the rider, having a clear goal to aim for).

- Motivation is a moveable and fragile state, which can be influenced by good or bad teaching, by a good or bad experience on the horse.

- Riders can be self-motivated or at times need to be motivated by others.

- Be aware of different coaching styles and where and when they may be relevant.

How to become competent (motivation, goal setting and coaching styles)

- Consider what goals you have set yourself, or had set for you, during your life but particularly with regard to your riding career.

- Goals must be appropriate or realistic for the rider concerned, they must be achievable and measurable. If they are not any of these things, then often they are unachievable and this in itself can be very demotivating if the goal is unattainable.

- Consider other trainers of riders and consider how they establish goals and what those goals are.

- Watch the outcome of the goal setting and realise that there are times when a goal may have to be adjusted (up or down) to take account of a change in circumstances (e.g. a horse goes lame and then a competition, which was planned, may have to be rescheduled or abandoned).

- Goal setting and motivation have some connection. Recognise that achieving a goal for a rider is very motivating and at that point a new goal should be set to keep the rider's interest and commitment.

- Ask riders (both those you may teach yourself and others) what drives them; find out what stimulates their enthusiasm.

- Also find out what lowers their motivation. It may be things like the winter, cold dark nights, and lack of someone with whom to share their interest.

- Watching top riders on television or video may motivate riders. Talking to other riders and sharing similar experiences may stimulate them.

- Try to watch lessons as often as you can and consider what the short-term goal might be for that lesson, whether it was clear at the beginning and whether it was achieved.

- Ask other instructors to clarify their sessional, short and long-term goals with a group of riders or an individual.

- Analyse your own coaching style and try to utilise other coaching styles at appropriate times.

Safety

When coaching riders safety must be your first priority. Clients put their faith in you and you should respect that by doing everything you can to ensure the safety of

BHS RISK ASSESSMENT

ACTIVITY ASSESSED

Hazard and severity (1 = minor, 2 = serious, 3 = very serious/fatal)

Risk (likelihood) (1= very unlikely, 2 = unlikely, 3 = likely/very likely)

Hazard x Risk = Hazard severity (1–3 = low, 4 or 5 = medium, 6+ = high)

HAZARD	AT RISK	CONTROLS	RISK RATING (RR)	OTHER PRECAUTIONS

both them and the horses they are riding. Many basic safety precautions have already been discussed throughout this book.

All lessons should have a risk assessment undertaken to ensure that all potential risks and hazards have been considered. The easiest way to undertake a risk assessment is to break down the lesson into sections/exercises, write them down and then consider the potential risks and hazards. Grade the risks 1, 2 or 3 and do the same for the hazards. If you multiply these two numbers together you will know how high the potential risk is. Within the risk assessment you must also note what you are going to do to minimise the risk.

Your experience coaching and round the yard will help you with highlighting where the high risk issues are. By discussing them with other involved parties (e.g. clients and helpers) you are already starting to minimise the risk.

Although it is essential to try and minimise the risk, there will occasionally be times when the unexpected occurs. It is essential that the coach has a knowledge of accident procedure. Whether it is in a ride or on the yard, the basic process is the same:

Firstly, stay calm and assess the situation. Never put yourself or others at further risk if an accident has occurred. There is no point in ending up with extra casualties.

Secondly, assess the casualty. Make sure they are not in any secondary danger. Talk to them as you approach. If they are crying or screaming that is better than them being silent. If they are silent they may be unconscious.

If they are still and silent, send somebody else to dial 999 (in the UK) and call an ambulance. Meanwhile you should go up to the casualty and check for a response. Call their name and give them a gentle shake on the shoulder.

Remember ABC:

• **Airway**: Open and clear the airway. Tilt the person's head backwards by lifting the chin up and supporting the head with your other hand. If they are wearing their riding hat, do not remove it. Check there are no obstructions in the mouth. This can range from false teeth to the tongue having slipped back.

• **Breathing**: Check that the casualty is still breathing. Do this by placing your ear near their mouth or check their ribcage for movement up and down. If they are not breathing you need to undertake CPR, for which you need specialist training. (If you have attended an Equine Specific First Aid Course or a four-day Health and Safety at Work Course, you will have practised these skills.)

• **Circulation**: Check the casualty still has a pulse by pressing two fingers on the carotid artery, which can be found by the windpipe on the neck. It is a good idea to practise finding this pulse on yourself so you know exactly where to feel for it on a casualty.

Keep the casualty warm until professional help arrives. Do not move the casualty unless you have to leave them alone. (The only time you would need to do this is if there is nobody else around and you have to leave to summon professional help. If this situation does arise then place the casualty in the 'recovery position'. This position ensures that the airway cannot become blocked.) If you are remaining with the casualty you will hear if the airway is starting to become blocked and can use your finger in the mouth to unblock it. It is important to only use the recovery position when absolutely necessary as moving the casualty could cause further issues if a spinal injury is involved.

If the casualty is conscious, assess the situation before making any decisions on what to do. It is important to keep the casualty still and talk to them to give reassurance. Ensure, by observing them, that they are not having any breathing difficulties. If there is an obvious major injury then send somebody to dial 999 for professional assistance. While you are waiting, if the casualty is bleeding then try and stem this by applying direct pressure. If an arm or a leg is bleeding then raising the limb above the level of the heart can slow this. If a limb appears to be at a peculiar angle or there is an obvious broken bone, then make every effort to keep the person still so that the issue is not compounded. Keep the casualty warm. Be self-assured to give the casualty and other people confidence.

It is absolutely vital that after every incident you fill out an accident report form or the accident/incident book as per the policy of the yard. If the casualty is a child then an insurance claim can be made up to three years after their 18th birthday. This could be a good many years, so accurate information is imperative. All the details should be recorded: date, time, names of rider and horse, exercises being undertaken and general facts about the incident. The weather should also be noted as should the names and contact details of any witnesses. Insurers advise centres not to take statements from witnesses, but to leave that task to them should the necessity arise. The insurers will then ensure that the language used by witnesses is not derogatory to the incident.

Any accident that involves a broken bone (other than a finger or toe) or hospitalisation, has to be reported to the local Environmental Health Department through RIDDOR, the Government body in charge of work-related incidents.

What the assessor is looking for (safety)

- The most important thing is to appear confident about what you should and should not do. The assessor would like to feel as if you were helping the situation, not exacerbating the issue.

- You must be able to talk confidently about basic care of casualties.

- You must stress the importance of calling for professional help.

- Remember to discuss the importance of accident reporting, what needs to be written down and why.

How to become competent (safety)

- The best way to become competent is to take either the BHS Equine Specific First Aid course or the four-day Health and Safety at Work course.

- Ask if you can read the accident report book to understand how to fill one in.

- Discuss the RIDDOR process with your proprietor.

Safeguarding Children and Vulnerable Adults

The candidate should be able to:

Show a basic understanding and awareness of child protection issues and the way in which these matters may impact on teaching at this level.

ELEMENT

C	**8.1.1** Explain the responsibilities imposed by 'duty of care'.
S	**8.2.1** Describe good practice.
S	**8.2.2** Describe poor practice.
C	**8.3.1** List indications of abuse.
C	**8.4.1** Give appropriate action in response to child abuse.

Why is Child Protection an issue?
- High physical risks
- Close proximity of instructors
- Physical contact
- Competitive atmosphere/pressure
- Elite athletes higher risk of abuse
- Can aid child protection because of possible close relationships forged

Who needs to be protected
- Children
- Riders with disabilities
- Riding instructors
- Volunteers

How can we protect them?

- British Equestrian Federation (BEF) Child Protection Policy
- BHS Instructors Register and Code of Conduct
- Good Practice
- Risk Assessment
- Safe recruitment procedures
- Training
- Accurate record keeping

Good Practice

- Ensure experience at equestrian events is fun and enjoyable
- Be an excellent role model
- Ensure that the training and competition intensity is appropriate to the physical and emotional development of the rider
- Conduct training and meetings in an open environment and avoid one-to-one coaching in unobserved situations
- Avoid unnecessary physical contact

Poor Practice

- Never take children to your home where they will be alone with you
- Never allow children to use inappropriate language unchallenged

Physical contact after a fall:

Get down to their level, check they are unhurt, and then, facing them, hold their hands in yours, look them in the eyes, squeeze their hands and reassure them it is alright and that everything is OK.

This is the safest and best method and is recommended by Sports Coach UK and the NSPCC.

Recognising Abuse

Physical signs

- Bruising
- Injuries
- Weight loss/gain
- Inadequate clothing, poor personal hygiene

Behavioural signs

- Aggression
- Introversion
- Low self esteem
- Delayed development
- Self harm

Incident reporting

Responding to the child

- Create a safe environment
- Be honest, never promise to keep secrets
- Record all the facts
- Maintain confidentiality but do not take on sole responsibility

Responding to allegations

- Discuss concerns with parents or carers
- Consult a senior collegue
- Consult/inform Governing Body Child Protection Officer (CPO)
- Inform social services/police
- Obtain medical attention
- Record everything

Clubmark

Background information

Clubmark is a mark of high quality clubs which helps to reassure parents, participants and local authorities that the club serves its participants well. Sports clubs that work with children and young people need and deserve support to improve the quality of work they do.

Benefits to clubs:

Its benefits include club development, increased membership, developing coaches and volunteers and an increased profile. The legitimacy to work with local authorities and other government agencies will also be enabled.

Benefits to participants

- Ensure the well-being of young people whilst in the care of adults, other than their legal parent(s)/carer(s)
- Enthuse young people to enjoy sport and active recreation to build a healthy and active lifestyle
- Enable young people to use their leisure time creatively
- Allow young people to optimise their talents and personal ability
- Identify and support the development of the most talented young people

What does it include

Clubmark accreditation involves completing a portfolio, which includes four sections plus an action plan:
- The Playing Programme
- Duty of care and child protection
- Sports equity and ethics
- Club management
- Action plan

Gathering the evidence is straightforward; each club is allocated a Clubmark officer and an assessor. The Clubmark officer will be there to support the club throughout the accreditation.

Further information

www.clubmark.org.uk

www.bhs.org.uk

What the assessor is looking for

- This will be covered in oral questioning in the theory section of the exam. There are likely to be five or six in each discussion group with one assessor.

- You should know that under a duty of care, you as the instructor in charge, should show a responsibility throughout all your time when working with clients for their safety and well-being (Element 8.1.1).

- You will ensure that at all times you work in the best interests of the clients' safety. (You ensure that they have help if needed with the horse they are leading/riding/mounting etc.)

- You understand that good practice is your ability to give a well-planned, well-delivered, clear lesson according to the needs of your pupil(s) whom you will have assessed.

- Good practice follows a safe code of behaviour based on good judgement and awareness of your pupil(s)' needs.

- You never choose work which they would not be capable of carrying out (which would endanger them). Poor practice would jeopardise your pupil(s)' safety and well-being (Element 10.2.2).

- Be able to consider what indications there may be of abuse (Element 8.3.1). The child may lose weight, may be more aggressive or tearful, there may be signs of physical bruising, this may be apparent if in the summer the child is in a short-sleeved shirt.

- Understand that your first responsibility is for the welfare of the child, but you must approach the issue with great sensitivity (Element 8.4.1).

- Always refer in the first instance to the senior member of staff to whom you are responsible.

- Beware of making any accusations without sufficient evidence, and even then be very careful to have a witness with you in the event that such discussion is not constructively received.

- You should be aware of the BEF incident reporting procedure which is available from the BEF *Safeguarding Children and Vulnerable Adults Manual*.

How to become competent

- Listen and learn, ask advice from other more senior instructors.

- Attend a safeguarding children and vulnerable adults course, run by the BHS (see appendix) where you will receive training on how to recognise and deal with children who might be suffering verbal, physical or emotional abuse from an adult.

- Consider the code of practice that exists in the establishment in which you teach or use the BEF code of practice.

- Consider how you should follow that code of good practice and conversely what would be considered as poor practice (e.g. good practice ensures that riders are never asked to attempt anything of which they are not capable or of which they feel apprehensive).

- Poor practice could be considered if a beginner rider were to be taken hacking and riding along a main road when their balance and coordination was barely established, and the instructor was chatting to her friend and using a mobile phone, with little or no regard for her pupil. (This scenario would completely lack good judgement and therefore the outcome would be poor practice.)

- Bear in mind that abuse could be considered if a rider were to be pressurised into working harder than their physical fitness allowed (e.g. if a beginner rider were to be expected to work for an entire lesson in trot without stirrups).

Portfolio Building

When you register for the PTT you will be sent a portfolio which you can work to complete. You can start to work on the portfolio before you take your PTT and certain work you undertake to prepare for your PTT forms an integral part of the document. You will also have the opportunity to register for the United Kingdom Coaching Certificate Endorsed Level 2 in Coaching.

The portfolio comes with concise instructions on how to complete all the sections and as to who can sign off the various sections. It also contains a number of appendices which can be used as proformas for the work you have to complete.

There are two parts to the portfolio. In **part one** of the portfolio you are required to:

Plan and prepare a series of four linked coaching sessions.

There are four tasks involved in this.

1. Identify, evaluate and record the needs of the rider(s) that you intend to coach.

For this you can use the rider registration form which is Appendix 1 in the portfolio or the rider registration form from your centre. There should be a copy for each of the riders in the group you are coaching.

You should black out their personal details before putting the sheets in the portfolio.

From this information you can analyse the needs of the riders and record them on a coaching participant record sheet. This is Appendix 2 in the portfolio. Again you should blank out their personal details and there should be a copy for each of your riders.

2. Produce coaching plans for the four linked riding sessions.

This is an outlined plan for the four linked sessions and should show that

- you have considered the resources that are required

- there is a logical duration and sequence for each session

- there is a suitable degree of intensity for each session

- you have considered your mode of delivery

- the technical content for each session is suitable.

For this you can use Appendix 3 in the portfolio.

You should then detail the plans for each individual session making it clear how you intend to break down the delivery of each of the sessions, identifying the aim of each of the activities that are going to be undertaken.

For this you can use Appendix 4 in the portfolio. There should be a plan for each of the four sessions. You can use your own lesson plan format if you prefer.

3. You need to demonstrate knowledge of suitability of horses.

For at least four of the riders involved in sessions you need to identify an ideal suitable horse for them to ride in the sessions. For this you can use Appendix 5, the horse suitability profile form.

4. You need to show evidence that you have planned for a safe coaching environment for each session.

For this you can use Appendix 6, which is a risk assessment form. You need to have one form for each session.

Part two of the portfolio looks at the actual coaching and the reviewing of it. There are two tasks in part two.

1. You will need to show that you have evaluated at least six sessions you have coached. You can use the evaluations of the two lessons in your PTT and then evaluate the four linked sessions you have prepared and given.

You will need to complete an evaluation form for each of the four sessions and for this you can use Appendix 7 in the portfolio. The other two sessions will be evaluated in Appendix 9, which will be completed at your PTT exam.

2. The second task is the formal assessment which will be completed at the PTT exam; the paperwork from this needs to be put into the portfolio after the exam. Appendix 8, the coach candidate report, will be completed by the assessor on the day of your exam and will be sent to you with the results. Appendix 9 will be completed by yourself and the assessor on the day and, again , will be sent to you from Stoneleigh with your results.

You also need to enclose copies of the lesson plans you have prepared for all the eight possible PTT lessons and all the notes you have prepared for the 6 lecture/presentations.

A copy of your PTT certificate should also be placed in the portfolio.

If you are using the portfolio to gain your BHSAI as well as your UKCC Endorsed Level 2 Coaching Certificate you must also place copies of your Stage 1,2, and 3 Horse Knowledge, Care and Riding in the portfolio along with a copy of the relevant first aid qualification and certificate of attendance from a Safeguarding and Protecting Children workshop.

Questions and Answers

Below are some basic answers to typical questions that assessors may ask.

- Remember that the questions are given as a guide only.

- Be confident that you can answer any question.

- Be sure that you have considered all the questions and feel able to add a little more information to each rather than just the minimal answer that is offered. The answer offered is to encourage you to do your own further research and to be able to expand your ideas on all subjects.

Business Knowledge

Q. A new client phones for information and to book a lesson. What information do you need to give? What information do you require from him/her?

A. Information you need to give:

What time lessons run.

How long the lesson is.

How much the lesson costs.

The number of riders in a lesson.

The standard of instructor taking the lesson.

The range of lesson types (lunge, lead-rein, class, private etc.).

The location of the establishment.

Specific information relevant to assessing new riders and introductory lessons to acquaint the new client with the centre.

Information from the client:

Past riding history, if any.

Age if under 18 (and approximately if adult).

Approximate height and weight.

What type of lesson they wish to take.

Q. Discuss ways of running an office regarding bookings, allocation of horses/ponies, payment and how it is recorded.

A. Here it may be appropriate to discuss the specific system that you have used in an establishment where you have worked or trained. E.g. Bookings taken by the secretary or person manning the office; liaison between the person running the office and the instructional staff to ensure that lessons are not overbooked; a senior member of the teaching staff who can mount clients according to their ability and standard of the lesson to make horse/pony allocation; payment made when the client arrives and record made in the day book with a forward booking taken at that time if required, etc.

Q. How do you encourage new clients to become regular clients?

A. Run a welcoming and friendly establishment.

Have horses/ponies that are gentle, pleasant to handle and well-schooled to ride.

Give encouraging lessons which stimulate fun, enthusiasm and learning.

Encourage groups of like-minded people of similar standard to ride together.

Offer incentives to riders to book ahead and arrange lessons in advance with a discount or free lesson for booking a number at a time.

Run any kind of social activity (school outing to Badminton) so that riders feel part of the establishment.

Q. What clothing is essential for beginner riders and how long would it be before you expected correct riding attire?

A. Safe footwear (sturdy shoes with a heel, not a ridged sole and preferably lace-up or zip shoes or boots – not trainers or wellingtons).

Trousers which are comfortable and not too tight-fitting.

No loose clothing, fashion clothing or jewellery.

Preferably gloves and a warm waterproof coat if outdoors and winter.

Correctly fitting riding hat which complies with current BSI standards for safety. (Possible to hire or borrow one from the establishment for two or three taster lessons.)

Gradually clients should be encouraged to own their own riding attire, starting with a hat.

Q. What is your policy when clients arrive unsuitably clothed or wearing jewellery?

A. If the school policy of advising clients before they arrive has been applied then it should not arise. If a client is unsafely dressed then this must be pointed out. It should be pointed out that excessive jewellery (dangling ear rings, bracelets etc.) might be damaged or could be a danger to the rider if it became caught (on this basis it is advisable to remove it). Basic safety – as in hat, shoes and trousers – must be adhered to in the interests of everyone's well-being.

Q. If lending BSI approved hats or body protectors to clients, what advice would you give on how they should fit?

A. Advise that you are not a qualified fitter. Advise that the hat/body protector should fit comfortably and stay in place without the person having to worry about it. Advise that the ultimate responsibility is with them to feel happy with the equipment and, if in doubt, they should provide their own.

Q. A new client wants to go for a hack and not have a lesson. Your policy is to assess everyone in a school or arena before allowing them to hack. How do you handle the situation?

A. Advise that the policy of the school is to assess and that it is for the benefit of the clients to ensure that they are safe to hack. Be polite but do not deviate from your rule, emphasising that your insurance policy requires that you are only able to allow clients to hack if they are deemed of a standard that the school has assessed as capable. A new client whether they are for lessons or hacking out must always complete a rider registration form.

Q. How many riders would you have in a class lesson? Does this depend on their standard? Would you use assistants or helpers and how would you brief them prior to the lesson?

A. A class lesson where much individual attention can be given consisting of four, six or eight riders is practical and increasingly viable economically. More than eight is acceptable, but requires a higher level of expertise on the part of the instructor to manage the bigger number, especially if the riders are of mixed ability or are less experienced.

Helpers can be an asset, particularly with novice riders or children who may need to be led or may need some individual help within the class. The helpers must be briefed to look to the coach for exact information throughout the lesson, according to the circumstances that arise.

Q. Is it practical to 'grade' riders so that class lessons contain riders of similar standards? Discuss and give the advantages and disadvantages.

A. It is usually an advantage to grade riders for class lessons. This enables riders to progress at a similar rate and is easier for the coach to manage. Some riders may still progress faster in spite of this policy, but this can provide an inspiration to others to try harder. Mixed ability rides are more difficult to teach to keep everyone challenged at their level and happy with their progress.

Q. Are children's holiday courses a good idea? Discuss.

A. Generally, yes. The children progress by spending a week handling, tacking up, riding and being around the pony/horse for a concentrated time. It is easy to progress to fun activities such as gymkhana games, handy pony competition and fancy dress, things that there would not be time for in usual weekly lessons. There does need to be an adequate number of staff to cover these courses.

Lesson Structure and Content

Q. What is meant by lesson structure?

A. A lesson that has a structure, has an aim, an introduction to that aim, a period of assessment and working-in when a choice is made on how to move the lesson forward. The lesson then has a period of work to develop the aim following through into a conclusion where the aim of the lesson is consolidated and the riders go away with confidence in what they have covered. During the conclusion there should be a summing up of the lesson and a plan for future lessons or some pointers to take away for the rider to think about or if possible work on for the future.

Q. How would your teaching differ for adults and children?

A. Children have a much shorter attention span.

Children have little inbuilt fear or anxiety about what 'might' happen so tend to be much more trusting of your expertise.

Children may be physically or mentally immature in their ability to control the pony/horse.

Adults tend to want to know more of the 'why' in doing things.

Adults have a greater awareness of 'how far it is to the ground!'

Adults may be physically less agile and supple.

Q. How would you prefer to start beginner riders? Lead rein, lunge, class, etc.

A. Lead rein is often good for small children where the contact is closer with the control of the horse/pony being taken by the leader. Very nervous adults will also benefit from lead rein lessons.

Lunge enables the teacher to have control of the horse but a good view of their pupil and the pupil can take some control of the horse as instructed. Some beginners find it hard to relax on the lunge.

Class lessons enable pupils to learn from each other and to gain confidence from each other.

Class lessons are more economically viable for a riding school.

Lunge lessons are labour intensive (one instructor/one pupil) and intensive on the horse.

Lead-rein lessons can be run with competent leaders under the control of one instructor.

Q. What teaching aids would you like to have available for lessons and lectures?

A. Cones, poles, small jumps (plastic jump blocks) for lessons.

Flip chart, white/black board, video, DVD. Good training books.

Q. How can lessons be kept interesting when the weather is bad and only a school or a manege is available for several months?

A. Involve the riders in pony/horse management sessions, grooming and tacking up prior to a lesson can teach stable-care skills and warm the riders up on a cold day.

Gymkhana games and 'handy' pony/horse exercises and gymnastic pole and jump work can all add to lesson variety.

Q. How can clients who prefer to hack out be encouraged to join lessons when the weather is too bad for hacking – and likely to be for some time due to ground conditions?

A. Run a simple competition within the school for clients in a basic riding (competence) test, basic stable management (perhaps some turn-out and plaiting) and encourage all clients to 'have a go'; this will encourage those who only hack to take some interest in the 'learning' of riding and care skills.

Have some kind of achievement badge, award, star system for clients who take a number of riding or stable management lessons.

Work clients towards the BHS Progressive Riding tests in the establishment.

Q. Exercises have to be taught and carried out well to be of benefit. Give examples.

A. Teaching basic school figures e.g. 20m circle and three-loop serpentine both require that the instructor shows the pupil clearly where the figure goes in the school. Using cones or markers to indicate the four points of a circle, or the points in the arena where the loops will pass, then enables the riders to ride accurately and they can then concentrate on the energy to sustain the pace and the rhythm of the pace.

The instructor may demonstrate himself or use one competent member of the class to show the rest of the class how an exercise should be ridden.

Q. When lungeing a rider what guidelines would you give as to holding – the reins (contact or not) the saddle, the neckstrap?

A. The rider should learn from the very first lesson how to hold the reins (as the reins are an essential part of the rider's aids and coordination so cannot be introduced too early).

At first the rider should learn to hold the reins with a fairly slack contact (leader or lunger will be in control of the horse). If necessary until they have their balance they can rest their hands on or hold the saddle at the same time.

Gradually the rider should be able to hold the reins and let go of the saddle first with one hand, then the other, then with both hands (first in walk only, then in trot).

The neckstrap should be there as a last resort, a 'grab' handle (rather than the horse's mouth).

Q. Explain what you mean by – and how you teach: half halt, turns and circles, impulsion, balance, diagonals, transitions, suppleness, forwardness, self-carriage, outline.

All these need careful study and understanding and the answers given below will only provide the briefest snapshot of a full answer.

A. Half halt is a preparatory aid which warns the horse of a further aid to come (e.g. half halt before riding a canter transition to warn the horse of the impending aid to canter). Teaching a rider about the half halt evolves through the rider's ability to 'prepare to' do something and by this apply their legs into a mildly containing hand which puts the horse's hocks under him and makes him more able to respond to the next aid.

Turns and circles. A turn is a change of direction through a 45-degree or 90-degree turn, a circle is a curved line sustaining a size of circle from 20m down to 15, 10 and 8m. The aids for a turn and a circle are similar; the aids for a turn are applied and then released after the turn, whereas the aids for a circle are applied for the duration of riding the circle (inside rein gives direction, inside leg maintains energy, outside rein controls the pace and the degree of bend and the outside leg controls the hindquarters with a position a little behind the girth).

Impulsion is contained or stored energy. The rider learns to generate the energy through the legs and a secure position is sustained through the seat and then they can regulate the energy they have created through their rein aids.

Balance is the horse's ability to carry his own weight and that of his rider over his four legs in whatever pace or movement is required of him to enable him to move with maximum ease and efficiency. Learning about balance comes with time and practice and developing feel for the horse underneath you.

Diagonals relate to the rider's position in rising trot relevant to the diagonal movement of the horse's legs. The rider must learn to recognise and ride on both diagonals in order to balance the horse on both reins in trot work. Developing the rider's awareness of diagonals is taught over a period of time and is easiest to start in walk, where the rider has time to watch the horse's shoulders moving forwards and backwards. As the shoulder moves back the foot is on the floor, as the shoulder moves forward, the foot is in the air. Transferring this to trot enables the rider to see which foreleg is on the ground as they sit in the saddle. If the left shoulder is coming back as the rider sits in the rising trot then the rider is sitting on the left diagonal. If the rider sits one extra beat in the trot they automatically change diagonal. This process takes time, patience and practice.

Transitions are changes of pace from a slower to a faster pace, from a faster to a slower pace or changes within a pace. They require preparation, clearly applied aids and a developing awareness of timing for the feel of the horse's balance. They are fundamental in the development of rider skill and the correct development of the horse's training.

Suppleness evolves from the horse's correct training and a harmony and balance in the way the rider rides the horse and communicates with him. Suppleness is impeded by a poorly balanced or uncoordinated rider.

Forwardness also evolves from correct training and riding. A horse that is trained to be responsive to the rider's aids and a rider who rides in balance and harmony will produce a situation where the horse is willing to go forward because it is easy for him to do so.

Self-carriage evolves from the horse's ability to carry himself correctly and in balance and with forwardness and suppleness.

Outline relates to the shape of the horse from his croup to his poll. It should be a rounded profile of a convex nature. The hind legs step under the horse, his back is rounded and forming a supple bridge between the activity of the hind legs, the carriage of the neck up from the shoulder and a submissive relaxed contact of the mouth through the elasticity of the poll and the jaw.

Q. What do you mean by jumping position or balanced seat when jumping? How do you develop it when teaching?

A. Adopting jumping position teaches riders a position which will help them to be in balance when the horse goes through the five phases of a jump (approach, take off, in the air, landing, getaway). The rider adapts his or her position to be able to stay in harmony with the horse as the horse changes his balance through these phases.

The rider adopts a slightly shorter stirrup length (one or two holes) and is then able to close the angles in the joints between foot and lower leg, lower leg and thigh and thigh and upper body. In this more closed position and taking the shoulders forward with a slightly shorter rein, the rider's seat moves back in the saddle and the rider covers a broader more flexible base position in the saddle, the seat is lighter and more weight is taken into the lower leg and heel which is deep and flexible. The rider is in a secure position to move in balance with the horse as he jumps.

The rider should work in jumping position in walk, trot and canter and over poles to establish confidence and security in this position before starting to jump.

Q. What are the advantages of using a grid?

(a) For horses

A. It develops the horse's confidence and athleticism in jumping. It can develop his suppleness in dealing with different distances.

(b) For riders

A. It develops the rider's confidence and ability while not having to worry about the distance between fences. It can bring the rider into exactly the right position for the jumps.

Q. Give examples of distances for ground poles and various ways of using them to the benefit of horse and rider.

A. Ground poles would usually be set at 4ft 6in (1.35m); these would be appropriate for trotting. Poles can be set singly or in groups of three or more to improve the rider's balance and accuracy to ride to the centre. The horse is improved in his early training in work over poles to develop, rhythm, balance and confidence.

Canter poles can also be used for more experienced horses and riders (set between 9ft/2.7m and 12ft/3.6m).

(a) A placing pole to a jump:

With a trot approach the pole would be at between 8ft (2.4m) and 9ft (2.7m).

With a canter approach the distance would be at least 9ft (2.7m). This would be for riders and horses with a great deal of experience – it would be less appropriate for novice riders. If using a canter pole with novice riders setting it at two canter strides away from the fence (approx. 30-33 ft [approx 9-10 m] is safer).

(b) For a bounce:

A bounce from trot would be 9–10 ft (2.7–3m).

From canter the bounce would be 10–12ft (3–3.6m).

(c) For a one non-jumping stride combination:

With a trot approach the distance would be about 18ft (5.4m).

With a canter approach the distance would be between 21ft (6.3m) and 24ft (7.2m).

(d) For a two non-jumping stride combination:

With a trot approach the distance would be about 28ft (8.4m).

With a canter approach the distance would be between 30ft (9m) and 33ft (9.9m).

Q. Explain what is meant by a related distance and how would you set it up when teaching. Give examples of distances you would use for three and four strides.

A. A related distance is two jumps, placed in such a way that when jumped one after the other there is a set number of strides in canter between the two jumps.

A three-stride related distance would be between 42ft (12.6m) and 48ft (14.4m).

A four-stride related distance would be between 51ft (15.3m) and 57ft (17.1m).

When teaching, develop the rider's feel for a good rhythm in canter and then start with two poles on the ground and help the rider to be able to feel or count the number of strides between poles. Gradually introduce jumps, keeping the first fence smaller while building up the second fence so that the rider finds it easy to jump in to the related distance with confidence and then build their ability to ride the related strides in a good flowing rhythm.

Q. Moving show jumps can be done with efficiency. Explain how you would carry wings and poles and how four or five fences can be erected quickly for a lesson, using one helper.

A. Keep all cups in a bucket so that they are safe and can be easily carried about and not lost on the floor.

Move heavy wings between two of you. Ideally, use light plastic equipment that is easily moved by one person.

Place poles at the site of where you want the jump and let your helper then bring the wings or blocks.

Choose a simple plan that keeps all the jumps in one area so that moving fences a long way is not time consuming.

If building a grid or combination, place it nearest the jump store, with the plain single jump furthest away.

Q. Is it important for once-a-week riders to have the same instructor each time?

A. The advantages would be that the riders would have confidence in the instructor with whom they are familiar. There is likely to be better continuity if the instructor knows the pupils and can relate to their weekly progress. The pupils are more likely to confide their hopes and fears to someone they know well.

The advantages of having a different instructor would be that a fresh eye can bring a new input or appraisal of the riders and different relevant exercises.

Q. Do you keep records of progress of riders? Are tests for clients appropriate?

A. It is wise to keep some records of progress for riders because then it is easier to follow through with progressive work especially if different instructors are taking the lessons. Rider registration forms must be updated regularly.

Tests for riders can provide a challenge and incentive to progress for riders. It can give them a bench mark of where they are in their riding compared to e.g. a year ago.

Q. How important is it to be aware of basic faults such as poor mounting and incorrect altering of stirrups, that creep in, despite initial correct teaching? Give other examples.

A. It is vital that a correct procedure is maintained and adhered to in all basic management and riding of the horse or eventually a casual fault will cause an accident.

Other examples: taking a coat off when mounted without either having someone hold the horse or being sure that you keep hold of the reins; lining up too close to other horses and allowing them to touch noses casually or swing their quarters towards each other; crowding horses together when leaving the arena (mounted or unmounted)

Q. You are planning an 'own a pony week'. What will you include and how will you ensure safety in the various tasks and riding activities?

A. One child per pony, each child to be monitored and supported by one instructor either directly if less competent or through a more competent member of the group who has experience of the type of day.

Include catching ponies (controlled and organised) grooming, tacking up, riding, untacking, cleaning tack, care of ponies after work. Some theory of pony care, some fun activity, mounted or unmounted, games or treasure hunt.

At all times the children must be supervised and the activities must be structured to ensure safety and organised fun.

Q. What are the Progressive Riding Tests? Can they benefit the riding school as well as clients?

A. Progressive Riding Tests are tests set by the BHS for adults and juniors to give them a gauge of their riding and stable management ability.

There are six tests for adults and five for juniors and these can be split into riding and stable management.

They can benefit the riding school by giving the school the chance to run courses and training aimed towards achieving the tests.

If all six adult tests are passed a rider can have direct access to the BHS Stage 2 exam.

Q. In a riding school where hacking includes some road work, would you encourage and train clients for the BHS Riding and Road Safety Test? What is involved?

A. The Riding and Road Safety Test is a useful addition to the training and knowledge of any rider who will ride on the public highway.

The test involves a comprehensive multiple-choice question paper on all aspects of road safety as delivered by the Highway Code, but with specific reference to horse riding. (All the relevant information can be found in The British Horse Society's booklet, *Riding and Roadcraft*, published by

Kenilworth Press.) There is also a ridden section on a simulated road, involving tests and hazards, and a further section which is assessed on a route set on a public highway.

Q. When a client asks you a question that you cannot answer, what do you do?

A. Ask a senior member of the establishment or your own instructor, or tell the person that you don't know the answer but will find out and come back to them on it.

Sports Psychology

Sample questions that should be discussed in the theory section.

Q. Discuss some qualities of a good instructor/coach.

A. Patience

Good knowledge and ability to put that across

Stamina

Good clear voice

Sense of humour

Enthusiasm

Confidence

Authority

Awareness

Fairness

Q. Why is feedback an important part of teaching?

A. Your pupils learn from the feedback that you give them.

They should be able to build on positive feedback.

It should give them a clear picture of where their strengths and weaknesses are and how to address them.

It allows for two-way communication between you and your pupil.

Q. What do you understand by the term 'motivation'?

A. Motivation is the 'drive' or incentive to want to do better.

Q. Discuss some ways you could motivate: (a) children, (b) adults, during a riding lesson.

A. Giving them a challenge to be better than each other often motivates children.

Giving them a specific aim, which they can all try to achieve, often motivates children (e.g. Who can get closest to the cone in the corner? Who can touch the cone from their pony?).

Adults may be motivated by a more individual aim (e.g. today we are aiming to canter for the first time).

Seeing someone else achieve the goal they are aiming for may motivate adults.

Q. How would you motivate riders who were not keen to ride?

A. Find out why they are not keen to ride. It may not be sensible to try to encourage them to ride if they really do not want to.

Riding is a sport that needs a degree of self-motivation.

Handling the horse and feeling more confident around him before riding him may encourage them.

It can help if they have ridden a mechanical horse, when they need have no fear of not being in control.

Q. What teaching methods could you adopt to motivate a class of teenage riders who have had to ride in the indoor school for several weeks due to bad weather?

A. Ask each rider to choose an exercise to explain to the rest of the class, and then the class ride it.

Make a mini competition on the best rider position, making them give themselves a mark out of ten (one being low and ten being high).

Do the same without stirrups and encourage them to improve on their own mark.

Do similar exercises but ask them to mark each other.

Q. What do you understand by 'goal setting' when teaching riders?

A. Goal setting is setting aims for riders which are achievable either in the sessional, short or long term. The goal must be measurable and realistic to the specific pupil.

A sessional goal might be to learn about diagonals in trot this week, a short goal may be to be able to recognise and change diagonal efficiently and a long-term goal may be to be able to feel which diagonal you are on on every horse you ride.

Q. Discuss the types of goal you could set for different riders (e.g. individual lessons in dressage or jumping, lead-rein lessons, class lessons, lunge lessons and stable management lessons).

A. The answer to this question could fill a small book in its own right. However, to help you answer this constructively in the exam, we will consider some options.

With all lessons the following criteria will help you to set the appropriate goals:

In a private lesson, consider the age and ability of the rider, how often they ride – so how fit they might be.

Ask them what they would like to do (in case they have a burning desire about something).

Consider the length of time you have to teach.

Consider the facilities you have. The goal for a novice child in a safe indoor school will be very different to the goal for that same child outside in a large field.

Consider the weather conditions. A lesson in walk on a hot day may be appropriate, whereas on a cold frosty day it would not.

Agree the goal with the rider. If the rider does not want to canter, that should not be your goal!

In a class lesson, there are other considerations such as whether all riders are of the same or similar ability, and, if you are likely to choose a jumping goal, whether all riders are mounted on horses/ponies that jump.

Lead-rein lessons are generally easier to set clear goals for, because you, as the leader, have total control over the pace of the horse/pony, which allows you to limit any problems that might arise.

Similarly, lunge lessons would usually be directed at some form of rider position improvement.

Stable-management lessons should be directed towards something that interests the pupil and helps them to be a more independent rider.

Listed below are one or two typical goals for each type of lesson.

Private dressage lesson. Improve awareness of rhythm in all three paces. Improve the basic transitions from one pace to another.

Private jumping lesson. Improve basic position using several fences in a simple grid. Improve the rider's ability to canter into a jump.

Lead-rein lesson. Improve the rider's confidence in going from rising trot to sitting to make a downward transition. Basic work without stirrups.

Class lesson. Improve the riding of turns and circles. Improve the knowledge of methods of changing the rein.

Lunge lesson. Improve the feel for the horse by identifying when the hind legs touch the ground. Improve the use of diagonals in trot.

Stable management lessons. Learning how to put on and fit tack.

Q. Consider each type of lesson and the type of goals you might set for an experienced rider and a more novice rider in the short and long-term situation.

A. The potential answers to this question are diverse and variable, and may be influenced by such things as the weather conditions, the confidence of the rider on 'that day', the frequency with which they ride, and other factors. The things to remember are that while planning and 'goal setting' are very important in any lesson, it is also vital that you teach 'what you see on the day' and do not stick rigidly to a plan or goal if that becomes unachievable due to an unforeseen reason.

- As a guide for an experienced rider in a class lesson:

  A **short-term goal** might be to work on the ability to slightly shorten and lengthen the horse's stride in trot, while working for a short period without stirrups to improve the rider's depth of position.

  A **long-term goal** might be to ride one specific horse to develop the range in all his paces, while linking the work to the development of lateral movements, which enhances the work further.

- For an experienced rider in an individual lesson:

  A **short-term goal** may be to understand the aids for turn on the forehand and to begin to be able to ride this movement.

  A **long-term goal** may be to have a greater understanding and feel for these movements and how they relate to the training of the horse and the feel for improving the paces.

- Choice of goals for novice riders would be much more aimed at consolidating the basic learning of things like:

  Basic correct position, balance and security.

  Basic understanding of the aids, how to apply them and how to develop coordination.

  Basic ability to ride transitions (simple transitions between each pace).

  Ability to ride simple turns and circles and to understand the basic principles of rhythm, suppleness, speed of the pace, contact between hand and leg, forwardness and balance.

Remember that for novice and experienced riders there are a range of experiences which can be included to develop their versatility and enjoyment as riders – for example, working in the school, in the fields, out hacking in the countryside, polework, jumping, independent riding (alone and in company). All these experiences could be built into any goal-setting programme.

Q. Imagine you are teaching a keen adult rider who has fallen off while jumping in a previous lesson and has lost their nerve. How would you proceed with your lesson/s to increase the rider's confidence?

A. Find out how they feel about the fall (whether they accept it was 'one of those things'/an occupational hazard, or are very negative about the circumstances of the fall).

Consider mounting them on a different horse on which they feel happy.

Go back to basic work in jumping position and over poles without any thought of jumping.

Wait until the rider actually wants to jump again before introducing a fence.

Work them in a group where other riders are addressing similar issues, so that the rider does not feel isolated in their own experience.

Q. If you are teaching a beginner rider who is not making much progress, what could you suggest to help to improve them?

A. ▪ Find out how they feel about their progress; it may not bother them that they are not making faster progress and so they are not trying particularly hard.

▪ Try to put them in a group where there are other riders of a similar standard so that may help to motivate them to progress as the others do.

▪ Perhaps change the instructor or the horse they ride.

▪ Perhaps suggest a lunge lesson or private lesson.

Q. What do you understand by the terms 'positive thinking' and 'negative thinking'?

A. People who think positively tend to see the bright side of things; they tend to be optimistic in their thinking and this can often affect their progress. They believe they are good and will tend to do better than negative thinkers, who are inclined to put themselves down and be pessimistic about their progress.

Q. How can positive thinking while (a) teaching and (b) riding affect your performance? Conversely, how can negative thinking affect a rider's and teacher's performance?

A. Consider this carefully and study some literature on sports psychology in the realm of positive/negative thinking. Consider your own attitude as both a rider and when teaching or being taught.

Q. How could you help the rider who has to ride a horse that no one else wants to?

A. Have a policy in the school that everyone rides every horse (according to their ability).

Encourage riders to see it is a positive advantage to develop their experience when riding something that is not liked.

Tell the rider that next week they can ride a horse of their choice.

Q. Can you give some reasons that may negatively affect a rider's performance?

A. Tiredness, illness.

Emotional problems (e.g. row with parent or boy/girlfriend).

Other worries (e.g. exams at school/college, money worries).

Fear of a past experience being repeated.

Q. Why do you think it is important to review a rider's performance at regular intervals?

A. To consider progress and make sure that the rider is progressing at an acceptable rate for them, taking all circumstances into consideration (e.g. how often they ride).

To ensure that the rider is happy with the agreed goals.

To reconsider the goals if some have been achieved and more need to be set.

Q. Clients like to feel valued. Why is this important and how can you ensure they do?

A. Everyone likes to feel valued, it is human nature.

Treat them as an individual (not as a number).

Know their name and speak to them personally whenever you can even if they are not one of your particular clients.

Involve them personally in decisions which affect them (goals, worries, progress).

Q. How can you encourage your clients to keep returning for lessons? What mechanism does the BHS provide to encourage riders to return for lessons?

A. Treat them as individuals.

Be interested in their progress.

Work out a personal plan for their development and needs.

Run classes and training days that appeal to what they want.

Have a club or loan horse system in your school which they can feel a part of.

The BHS runs the Progressive Riding Tests which your school can utilise in many ways to stimulate learning, enthusiasm for lessons and training.

A BHS approved establishment should offer a well-run centre in which a rider can develop their passion for their sport of riding.

Safeguarding children and vulnerable adults

Q. What is meant by the term 'duty of care'?

A. It is the adult's responsibility when in charge of children, to provide a safe environment for them in whatever activity they are involved.

The adult has a duty to provide as safe a situation as is possible for the welfare and well-being of any child.

Q. What age group is 'legally' classified as a 'child'?

A. Individuals up to the age of eighteen.

Q. Why is it important for riding instructors and coaches to have awareness of child protection issues?

A. Riding is a very physical sport and there are instances when a riding instructor may make contact with a child (e.g. legging up the rider, going to a rider who has fallen off and is distressed).

The position of the instructor in relation to helping a child must never be in question.

The relationship between child and teacher must always be of unquestionable integrity.

Q. What do you understand by 'good practice'? Give some examples of good practice when working with children.

A. Good practice is carrying forward training that is within the capability of the pupil(s) following a clear pathway of progress with clear explanation of work and much opportunity for the pupil to feed back on satisfactory progress.

Good practice with children would include clear but short explanation of work without overloading or confusing the child with information.

Short sessions of work so that the child is not bored or over-tired by the lesson.

Opportunity for two-way communication with the child to monitor progress and feedback.

Q. What sort of things should be avoided as poor practice?

A. Overwork so that the child is tired or disillusioned.

Over-criticism so that the child feels inadequate and disappointed.

Q. What special considerations or care must be taken when teaching children as opposed to adults?

A. Children may not be brave enough to tell you that they are cold, wet or tired.

Children may not be brave enough to tell you that they are afraid to do something or that they do not understand.

Q. Do you think it is a good idea to allow parents to become involved in their children's lessons?

A. It can be helpful if it is well controlled and the parents do not interfere (e.g. small child being led by parent although the instructor controls the lesson).

It can be detrimental if the parent takes over the lesson or the parent is saying one thing and the instructor another.

Q. What sort of problems could be caused by parents who are over-anxious about their child's safety?

A. They make the child more insecure and doubting of their own ability.

They cause disruption for other members of the class.

They affect the attitude of other parents.

Q. How would you deal with parents who are too pushy or over ambitious?

A. Firmly! Talk to them privately about the standards that the establishment sets and explain that you as the professional instructor rely on them to trust your ability and leave you to make the choices about what their child does or does not do in a lesson.

Q. What sort of things might cause you to have concerns about the welfare of a child in your ride?

A. A change in behaviour from normal (child normally outgoing becomes withdrawn or tearful).

Inconsistent behaviour or attendance from a normally consistent child.

Signs of physical abuse such as unexplained bruising on arms or face.

Q. What would you do/whom would you contact if you had concerns about the welfare of a child in your ride?

A. You must be very careful in your approach.

First you should discuss the situation with the parent or guardian of the child.

You might speak to a close friend (adult).

You might consider talking to a member of the staff at the school that the child attends.

Q. What would you do if one of the children in your ride or on the yard was being bullied or verbally abused by the other children?

A. If you see it actually happening then you must deal with the culprit and in doing so you must involve the parents of that child and if necessary ban the child from attending lessons in future until the behaviour is guaranteed to change.

If you only suspect it is happening, then you must try to get the confidence of the child being bullied or a friend who will give you the necessary evidence to tackle the issue.

You cannot act on hearsay and in every situation must deal very carefully with the circumstances.

Q. Where can you get information and advice on teaching people with disabilities?

A. Through the Riding for the Disabled Association. There is a national office and then most regions have a local group who would be able to offer local knowledge and assistance.

Q. How is it possible to protect children and vulnerable adults?

A. It is possible to safeguard by adopting the BEF Child Protection Policy and BHS Instructors Register and Code of Conduct. There are also helpful tools such as Risk Assessment, safe recruitment procedures, staff training and accurate record keeping. All instructors should work using good practice procedures at all times.

Q. Where can you get further information from?

A. NSPCC, CPSU and BEF member body lead welfare officers which can be found by contacting the BEF.

Further Information

Useful contacts

Child Protection in Sport Unit (CPSU)
0116 234 7278
www.cpsu.org.uk

NSPCC helpline
0808 800 5000
www.nspcc.org.uk

British Equestrian Federation
02476 698871
www.bef.co.uk

The British Horse Society
01926 707700
www.bhs.org.uk

Further Reading

The following books and booklets can all be obtained from the BHS Bookshop.

The BHS Complete Manual of Horse & Stable Management

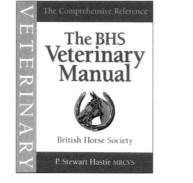

The BHS Veterinary Manual

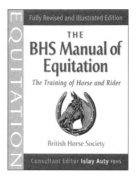

The BHS Manual of Equitation

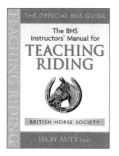

The BHS Instructor's Manual for Teaching Riding

The BHS Complete Training Manual for Stage 1

The BHS Complete Training Manual for Stage 2

The BHS Training Manual for Stage 3

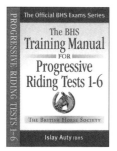

The BHS Training Manual for Progressive Riding Tests 1-6

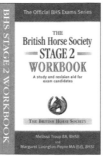

The BHS Stage 1 Workbook

The BHS Stage 2 Workbook

The BHS Riding and Roadcraft 12th Edition

Guide to BHS Examinations

Examinations Handbook

BHS Guide to Careers with Horses

BHS TREC

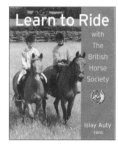

Learn to Ride with The British Horse Society

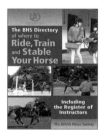

The BHS Directory of Where to Ride, Train and Stable Your Horse

Useful Addresses

The British Horse Society
Stoneleigh Deer Park
Kenilworth
Warwickshire
CV8 2XZ
tel: 0844 8481666 or 01926 707700
fax: 01926 707800
website: www.bhs.org.uk
email: enquiry@bhs.org.uk

BHS Bookshop
(address as left)
tel: 08701 201918
        01926 707762
website: www.britishhorse.com

BHS Standards Directorate

BHS Examinations Department
(address as above)
tel: 01926 707784
fax: 01926 707800
email: exams@bhs.org.uk

BHS Training Department
(address as above)
tel: 01926 707820
        01926 707799
email: training@bhs.org.uk

**BHS Riding Schools/Approvals
Department**
(address as above)
tel: 01926 707795
fax: 01926 707796
email: Riding.Schools@bhs.org.uk

BHS Competitions Department
(address as above)
tel: 01926 707831
fax: 01926 707796
email: competitions@bhs.org.uk

The BHS Examination System

Outline of progression route through
BHS examinations

EQL QUALIFICATIONS & BHS EXAMINATIONS

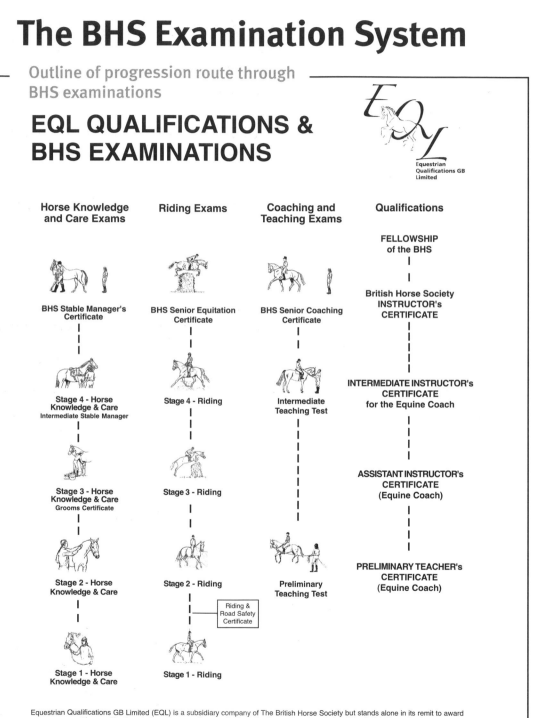

Horse Knowledge and Care Exams	Riding Exams	Coaching and Teaching Exams	Qualifications
			FELLOWSHIP of the BHS
BHS Stable Manager's Certificate	BHS Senior Equitation Certificate	BHS Senior Coaching Certificate	British Horse Society **INSTRUCTOR's CERTIFICATE**
Stage 4 - Horse Knowledge & Care **Intermediate Stable Manager**	Stage 4 - Riding	Intermediate Teaching Test	**INTERMEDIATE INSTRUCTOR's CERTIFICATE** for the Equine Coach
Stage 3 - Horse Knowledge & Care **Grooms Certificate**	Stage 3 - Riding		**ASSISTANT INSTRUCTOR's CERTIFICATE** (Equine Coach)
Stage 2 - Horse Knowledge & Care	Stage 2 - Riding	Preliminary Teaching Test	**PRELIMINARY TEACHER's CERTIFICATE** (Equine Coach)
	Riding & Road Safety Certificate		
Stage 1 - Horse Knowledge & Care	Stage 1 - Riding		

Equestrian Qualifications GB Limited (EQL) is a subsidiary company of The British Horse Society but stands alone in its remit to award equestrian qualifications to the same exacting standards as the former Awarding Body of The British Horse Society.